MW01041917

Red arrow

Love, Death & Tango

A Buenos Aires Memoir

Maraya Loza Koxahn

Loza-Koxahn, Maraya, 1958 –
Love, Death & Tango: A Buenos Aires Memoir

All events are true (mostly); a few names have been changed.

Cover photo & design—John Heerema
Published by The Book Babas
Printed by Blitzprint
Calgary, CANADA

Also available in print or e-book through KDP Kindle

ISBN 978-0-9737957-7-6

www.TheBookBabas.com

For all Tangueros seeking Nirvana.

Relative increases in testosterone boost a woman's spatial awareness and augment her sense of direction. A wanderlust that she never had earlier in her life often seizes her, and she embarks on pilgrimages to distant places or travels to exotic locales, intent on seeing the world and having adventures.

Leonard Shlain, *Sex, Time & Power*

CONTENTS

Love, Death & Tango

PROLOGUE

Sunrise over the Andes sliced through my eyelids and hijacked my breath. Too soon. I wasn't ready to start the future. I preferred to remain suspended at 35,000 feet—going somewhere, never quite there—safe inside my seat belt just a little longer. I pulled the shade down and squeezed my eyes shut, attempting to stop time.

Time was slipping away from me. My life wasn't particularly bad, I lacked for nothing. In fact, it was pretty good; yet, I was rarely satisfied for long. Being satisfied tended to keep me standing still; I wanted to keep moving. I had the feeling there was something missing, something more, something yet undone, something that would fulfill me. I needed to find it. By fifty, I should be able to do what I damn well pleased, so I decided to celebrate my golden birthday alone. I didn't like to be fussed over. I packed in a career, bought a new suitcase, and planned a sabbatical from my everyday life.

Shortly after my second divorce, I'd been struck by my accumulation of "mistakes" and by thoughts of mortality. In my mind's eye, I caught a glimpse of my epitaph: *She never danced enough*. Feeling compelled to change that prophecy and reduce my regrets, I enrolled in ballroom dance classes. It would be a healthy distraction and a good way to meet men. From there, I was introduced to Argentine Tango by male members of that dance community trying to solicit new partners. Intrigued, and after a little research, I was hooked before my first lesson. It promised such passion.

I found a partner through a mutual friend and together we began a journey to learn this complex dance. A few years into that journey, Don had an opportunity to go to Buenos Aires for work. Even though both of us had just begun romantic relationships with other people, I couldn't imagine not accompanying him. In fact, I insisted. He was happy to oblige. We were convinced that we were mature enough to travel together to the Motherland of Tango and remain true to our lovers back home.

I fell in love with the "Paris of the South," with its gritty history embedded in European architecture and its Latin-flavoured culture spilling out into the streets. Don fell in love with me. We returned home to our respective partners, but the city had captivated me and surreptitiously drew me back.

The cabin lights officially announced the arrival morning and the flight attendants bustled about with breakfast. The plane would stop in Santiago before the final leg across the continent to the capital of Argentina. I raised the shade to a spectacular view of dawn-tinged, snow-dusted mountains: strangely diminutive yet collectively powerful from my vantage point. These mountains were new to me, but not unlike the Rockies in Western Canada. I pulled out my camera to begin recording my journey while my awe of the view, and excitement about the ensuing adventure, wedged into my psyche. I turned back toward the window of the airplane to hide wet cheeks from fellow passengers. I'd done it. I'd run away from home.

Ж

Buenos Aires welcomed me back with a warm, humid embrace. After collecting my luggage, I hustled through immigration without a hitch—there were no questions about my one-way ticket. I secured a taxi at the kiosk inside the airport terminal in order to avoid potential shysters waiting outside.

Within five minutes, my taxi came around to collect me. The driver seemed undeterred by my statement that my Spanish was only *mas o menos* and kept speaking to me as we drove the forty minutes into *el centro*. *Taxistas* have their fingers on the pulse of a city and can be a wealth of useful information, but I felt insecure about my language skills and too tired to practice. I would have plenty of time to find out what was going on in the city.

I drifted in and out of my thoughts and sponged up the view outside my window, while keeping an ear available for what might be a question I'd be expected to at least attempt to answer. I should have told him in English, not Spanish, that I was inept, because even with limited vocabulary, my ability to mimic a Spanish accent, and my dark features, sometimes pegged me as a *latina*.

It was comforting to return to the familiar tango house where Don and I had stayed two years prior. Casa de Pilar was on a quiet cobble-stone side street, just a block from Avenida Rivadavia—believed by Argentines to be the longest avenue in the world—and close to the exquisite Las Violetas Restaurante.

Pilar, the owner of the guest house, was expecting me since we had confirmed my arrival by email. I paid the *taxista*, pulled my luggage into the alcove of the gated, century-old *casa*, and rang the bell. Diana, who occupied the bedroom across from the front door, answered and recognized me from two years earlier. Still with no English, Diana greeted me in Spanish.

"*Hola Maraya, ¡qué sorpresa! ¿Cómo estás?*"

"*Muy bien, ¿y tú?*"

"*¡Bien!*"

"*¿Pilar está?*"

Pilar wasn't there. It seemed she'd forgotten about my arrival. Having gotten to know her somewhat over the two weeks I'd lived there previously, I wasn't surprised; she was slightly scatterbrained. Diana called Pilar at her home nearby then indicated to me that it wouldn't take her long to arrive by bicycle. While I waited, I surveyed my surroundings. Not much, if anything, had changed except maybe two more years of dust and clutter. The *salón* had a small tiled dance floor with a large mirror on the wall, and the same strange eclectic mix of knick knacks as before. Still, it felt comfortable, familiar, and was now the closest thing I had to home.

Pilar seemed flustered when she arrived and, after brief niceties in Spanglish, led me, fresh linens in hand, halfway up the back stairs from the kitchen to a small bedroom that must have been the maid's quarters at one time. At the top of those stairs was the bedroom Don and I had shared—platonically. That bedroom opened up onto a huge disused rooftop patio where we'd danced a tango one night under a full moon.

Pilar made the bed and left me to unpack enough for a two-day stay. I was glad to have a real bed after too many hours asleep in an airplane seat, but I was still too wired to sleep. Pilar, one of Buenos Aires' many psychotherapists, had filled her shelves with books about psychotherapy and related subjects. I cocked my head to read the Spanish titles and chose one that intrigued me. It was a fictional account of the therapeutic relationship between Friedrich Nietzsche and Joseph Breuer—who had once been a mentor to Sigmund Freud. The book appeared to be a marriage of psychology and philosophy with a twist of history and fiction. I opened the front cover of *El Día Que Nietzsche Lloro*[1]* to test my Spanish:

> *Hay quienes no pueden aflojar sus propias cadenzas y sin embargo puedan liberar a sus amigos. Debes estar*

[1]Yalom, Irvin D., 1992.

preparado para arder in tu propio fuego. ¿Cómo podrías renacer sin haberte convertido en ceniza?

Asi hablo Zarathustra.

I understood the quote to mean: There are those who cannot loosen their own chains even though they can free their friends. You should be prepared to burn in your own fire. How will you be reborn without becoming ashes? Thus spoke Zarathustra.

Perfect. Bring it on.

CHAPTER 1

Loosening the Chains

I'd had a dream. Before my first marriage, I'd worked as a travel consultant. In the quiet times, I would plan my dream trip with semi-seriousness. Tierra del Fuego was the name that had tickled my tongue and my imagination. With that ironic name for the southernmost tip of the Americas—El Fin del Mundo—the Land of Fire was the leaping-off point for frozen Antarctica. But, I got married and the dream went into a coma. Marriage quelled my fire, but my *desire* for fire continued to smoulder beneath the surface, awaiting the opportunity to ignite like a grenade.

Ж

If I don't move…everything will be okay….

They're called heavy-duty, overnight maxi-pads, in an attempt to instill a sense of security with the name, but I'm not fooled. They're not as reliable as gravity. Menstrual blood hasn't got the same viscosity as television commercials' blue water; it's not easily absorbed. Having slept fitfully, I lay semi-awake, luxuriating in the comfort of my flannel sheets, and reluctantly contemplated rising to contend with a probable mess. Finally forced to my feet, I dashed to the bathroom with squeezed pelvic-floor muscles. Too late.

I stripped, put my pyjamas in the sink, ran cold water, and went back to my bedroom to see if I had to change the sheets. By the time I returned to the bathroom, there was water all over the floor from the overflowing sink. It looked like a crime scene. I'd only been awake for five minutes and already my day was a B grade comedy. I almost laughed at my predicament. Almost. The "change" is a bitch.

I descended the stairs and turned up the thermostat, went into the kitchen, filled the kettle and plugged it in. While I waited for the water to boil, I chose a lemon from the fridge, sliced it in half, squeezed the juice into my favourite mug, added a tablespoon of maple syrup and filled it with hot water. My healthy start to the day usually spiralled down from there.

I heard Amy, my younger daughter, moving around in her bedroom. It used to torture us both when I tried to coax her into consciousness so she could eat breakfast and get to school on time. After much cajoling, pleading, guilting, fighting, and frustration, I decided she was old enough to suffer the consequences of broken agreements with the school and I was old enough to let go of that responsibility. She could choose to get to school on time or not. I was perfectly willing to drive her in nasty weather but no longer willing to have her hate me for shortchanging her sleep. I wanted her to evolve into an adult so I backed off. Tough love.

"Mom, can you give me ride?" Amy yelled through the closed door.

"Sure."

"I have a test."

"Okay."

Always without eating, but never without careful make-up application (her not me), we bolted out the door. I tried to engage her in conversation but it was futile as usual. She typically didn't express interest or appreciation, only entitlement and disdain. She was particularly good at disdain. Amy dashed from the car and into the school without a word of thanks.

My sixteen-year-old was teaching me patience. She'd been caught shoplifting at the mall with her friend (a bad influence) and they weren't allowed to set foot in there for six months. Her grades had deteriorated and my ex and I had hired a math tutor for her. She slept a lot, rarely spoke to us, and hung around doing nothing, or whatever it is that teenagers do. Her dad and I had sent her to summer camp to ride horses and hike and do other outdoor activities with kids her age. We actually *forced* her to go, hoping it would shake her up, change her in a good way, but it didn't appear to have had an effect at all. She didn't tell us a damn thing about it when she returned and acted like she hated us for having sent her. Still, we were hopeful. Her sister had successfully matured out of the terrible teens and I expected Amy would too. Eventually.

Amanda, my first-born, had recently returned home from her second attempt at playing house with her boyfriend. She was going to college and working at Starbucks and didn't want to live with her father either. So, after many years of shared parenting, I had both girls. I loved them dearly; I even liked them. At times, they'd been my only reason to stay on the planet. But, I'd been a single mom part-time for fifteen years and I was tired.

I'd been in a relationship of one kind or another since I'd met my daughters' father at the age of fifteen. I had essentially gone from my marriage to him into another and, having failed a second time, bumbled through several short-term relationships. I suffered from chronic disappointment. I didn't want the responsibility of a man in my life. At least that's what I told myself to partly justify leaving the relationship I was then in.

My career had devolved from Wholistic Therapist to just Massage Therapist. My job no longer challenged me and my creativity was suppressed. I felt stuck; I was bored. It was time to retire from taking care of others. I had to extricate myself from the endless tangle of obligations, expectations, appointments, errands and chores. I had to leave monotony and predictability. I needed adventure.

I knew a geographical cure wasn't the answer. My ex-husband, the antithesis of a pundit, used to say, "No matter where you go, there you are." There was no escaping myself. But maybe I could take a well-deserved and much-needed pause from men and re-evaluate my decision-making criteria. Maybe I could figure out my next career. A sojourn was rife with hope and possibility.

After dropping Amy off at school, I did some errands. While I stood in front of the display of travel brochures at the AMA, waiting to talk to an insurance agent, I was attracted to a brochure littered with pictures of penguins. I picked it up. Inside, there was a picture of a couple dancing tango. South America called to me. Oxygen was available. A spark ignited deep inside me; I was combustible. I would go to The Land of Fire.

CHAPTER 2

Fatherless Daughters

*Life is what happens to you
when you're busy making other plans.*

John Lennon

Preparing for a trip of such magnitude took a lot of planning and tidying up of loose ends. I hadn't yet settled on a departure date but it would have to be several months hence. I'd have to find a renter for my condo. I brushed up on my Spanish and took a workshop to learn how to teach and tutor ESL. I even applied for a position as a tour guide so I could work my way around the continent. My ex would have to agree to take responsibility for the girls full time. Since Amy had successfully graduated from high school and nobody was in crisis, I could escape soon. I aimed for fall. But, "life" had other plans....

Ж

My daughters must have suspected bad news from the tone of my voice on the phone when I insisted they cancel their plans and come straight home. They hadn't asked questions.

I had been visiting my friend Solarius at the Rockyview Hospital earlier in the day. He was a rebellious forty-year-old man: tall and slim, with long, dark, curly, and lightly salted, hair. Always dressed in black, his body gnarled by Cerebral Palsy, he didn't fit the image of the typical massage therapist that he'd been. He was intelligent and cynical and not afraid to say what he thought. We were neighbours and enjoyed hanging out together since he'd moved to "Boomtown" to strike it rich in the trades as an aspiring electrician.

Since he'd blamed allergies for his persistent cough, Solarius hadn't bothered to get checked out until he started spewing blood. Too late. What began as lung cancer, insinuated itself into his bones and was already on its way to his brain by the time of my visit. He'd deteriorated rapidly but was still hopeful. He insisted on fighting as he had for most things in his life.

I returned home late that summer afternoon from the hospital and slumped down at my desk to process the previous few hours. The phone startled me. My ex-husband's sister was calling from Edmonton. No small talk. In a split second I expected bad news about my elderly mother-in-law.

"Are you sitting down?" she asked.

"Yes," I replied.

"Gerry's dead."

That, I had not expected.

I never imagined, especially after more than fifteen years of divorce, that I would have to tell my daughters their father had been killed.

Ж

I was familiar with the pain of the early loss of a father. It can define the life of a young woman, as it did mine. Thirty-five years earlier, my mother had silently walked through our front door after visiting my father in the hospital. She looked at me with pain in her eyes; she didn't have to say a word. Our battle with cancer was over.

We had been the perfect family; we'd "made" it. My father had been a well-paid, well-respected, Petroleum Engineer; my mother was a part-time Pharmacist; my younger brothers and I were three healthy, happy children. We lived in a substantial brand-new home, designed by my father, in a desirable new Calgary suburb.

Maybe it was worse for my mother to have to tell me at the beginning of the ordeal. We'd been doing the dinner dishes together only a few months earlier. I was thirteen.

A first false diagnosis of Hepatitis C turned out to be a more formidable "C"—a disease I didn't think I had any knowledge of. Maybe it was the tone of her voice, or maybe it was because she didn't say everything was going to be okay, that convinced me it wasn't. When Mom simply stated, "Your father has cancer," I somehow knew it was a death sentence.

Stunned into silence, I put down my towel and retreated to my pink and white bedroom upstairs. I had often stared out my window and imagined myself to be Juliet overlooking the park below, waiting for Romeo to arrive. I stood motionless by the window as tears streamed down my cheeks. My life as I had known it, with its fragile "perfect family" veneer, was shattered. No one was coming to rescue me.

Ж

My daughters sat side by side on the couch with me on the floor in front of them. I began to crumble before I could even speak. I simply uttered, "Your dad is dead," as they joined me in a sobbing heap.

Amanda opened up with a wail, "Noooo!"

Amy, more like her mother, shut down.

It was a moment I wanted to edit out of our lives. However, we would have to learn to endure together.

Ж

Shortly after my father died, my mother sold our dream home and we moved to Edmonton from Calgary to be close to family. In only a few months I'd lost my dad, my home, my school and my friends. It was the seventies and we didn't know how to "heal" our trauma. We didn't even know we needed to. Part of me turned to stone. I shut down my emotions and tried to fit in to my new environment. I wasn't even able to utter the word "dad" for the longest time. I was shy and insecure in school. I was offended and resistant when Mom suggested I might benefit from talking to a therapist. Not many people considered that children needed grief support in those days. We were pretty much left to figure it out on our own. It took half a life to heal. I survived and thrived and nothing would ever hurt me like that again. The death of my father at such a vulnerable age—when I needed feedback about my blossoming womanhood—informed many of my major life decisions.

At the age of fifteen, while walking through our townhouse complex one day, I was greeted by a boy driving a brand new 1973 *Basin Street Blue* Challenger. It was a cool car.

Gerry was nineteen and, literally, the boy next door. I didn't like him at first. I thought he was a greaser. But, he was nice and he started to grow on me. The fact that he was older, out of high school, and had a job and a car, was rather attractive to a girl who needed some kind of a father replacement. My boyfriend was fun, funny and kind, and he was crazy about me.

Gerry and I were together for the greater part of ten years before we got married. We moved to Calgary and I became pregnant right away, during my first year of university. Our second daughter was conceived the day I graduated.

My days consisted of balancing family life with satisfying my need for intellectual and creative stimulation. I probably should've gotten a job but my high school education wouldn't have awarded me anything satisfying, and would have just further sucked my soul.

Art school was an expansive experience for me. Consequently, I outgrew my husband. His world consisted of stereotypes attributed to Western Canadian oil patch employees. I was anxious to be free of my restrictive middle class, big "C" Conservative, and Christian, suburban lifestyle. A second child did little to keep us together. Before Amy was a year old, we separated.

Gerry and I struggled for years, sharing the responsibilities for our children. In spite of our extreme differences, if we kept our discussions focused on the girls, we managed to have a workable relationship, most of the time. We both remarried and Gerry renewed his passion for motorcycles.

It had been a beautiful clear August day when Gerry set out on his Harley toward the 2007 Sturgis Motorcycle Rally in South Dakota with five of his buddies. Shortly after breakfast in Helena, Montana, he just rode off the road. There had been no warning, no indication that he'd been in any kind of distress, physical or mechanical. He'd always been a careful and skilled rider.

The coroner stated the obvious: Cause of death was trauma to the head. Gerry's widow saw no need for an autopsy. As the mother of his children, I'd have preferred an accurate medical history, but as the ex, I didn't have a say. However, I didn't need a coroner's report to know that Gerry's cardiovascular system had long been compromised. I knew his history and his symptoms; I'd known Gerry longer and better than almost anybody except for his family of origin. Although he appeared jovial, like the good salesman he was, I sensed he was fundamentally unhappy. He was overweight; he'd been the victim of two previous motor vehicle accidents in which he'd sustained head trauma; he'd suffered headaches and insomnia for years. More recently, I'd noticed strange changes in his behaviour. I believed that the external head trauma had been preceded by internal head trauma, perhaps an aneurysm. I believe he was unconscious, if not dead, before he hit the ground.

I'd thought, at times with annoyance, that Gerry would always be around. Even though sometimes it didn't seem like it to us, I knew that his family was what mattered to him most. All his peers, colleagues, family, and friends knew he was, overall, a responsible and reliable man. We all counted on him.

Bastard. I was furious with him for making his hasty exit, for leaving us to clean up his mess, for leaving his daughters fatherless. Anger proved to be only part of my grief. There had been so much animosity between us that I hadn't realized there was still love … or something like it.

Amy insisted her father be buried in a cemetery. He hadn't discussed the matter with his second wife, but I believed he'd have wanted a traditional send-off. The girls and their stepmother scrambled to find him an appropriate resting place, a place where they could go to remember him, talk to him, and grieve. They found the perfect plot west of the city, on a hill overlooking the Rocky Mountains.

The wall-to-wall attendance at his funeral was a testament to his popularity. Gerry was revered by almost everyone who knew him. He looked uncharacteristically pale and peaceful in his coffin, dressed in a short-sleeved tropical-print shirt chosen by his daughters. Gerry died doing what he loved and would spend his eternal vacation on a small piece of land west of town like he'd always wanted. I think he was finally happy.

A week after Gerry's funeral, Solarius died.

CHAPTER 3

It's Just a Lump...

When we moved to Edmonton after my dad died, I entered grade nine at the start of the school year: the new girl. A few weeks into the semester, Nicki walked into my homeroom. We ended up sharing a locker and becoming best friends. Even though she was half a year younger than me, she was older in experience. Born in England, and having grown up in Vancouver, she was the more-worldly one. She introduced me to drugs and we skipped classes together to expand our minds. Only three years later, her dad died too. By then, she had dropped out of high school and, for the most part, we'd lost contact.

Over the years, Nicki and I drifted in and out of each other's life. We had both moved around Western Canada, and once in a while we'd seek out each other to catch up about the latest husband or other love interest, career move, or workshop experience. We had both turned away from drugs and toward personal and professional development, spirituality, and metaphysics to expand our minds. We shared a mutual, non-judgmental respect and similar open-minded beliefs. I had no sisters and only a few good friends. Nicki was the best of them.

We looked like Mutt and Jeff together. Her curly dark hair showed its age, whereas I kept my fine hair straight, short and spiky, and coloured. Even with breast reduction surgery, Nicki would always be more voluptuous than me; I was the willowy one. For as long as I'd known her, she'd worn some version of the first blazer she'd made in Home Economics class in grade nine. She always seemed dressed up, more business-like, prim and proper, very "British." I couldn't remember the last time I'd seen her in jeans. In contrast, I almost always wore jeans. I was once told we had a past life connection where I had been a Samurai warrior and she'd been my younger sister. That may have explained why I still felt protective of her—not that she needed it. She was one of the most independent women I knew.

Nicola, as she now called herself, had recently returned to Calgary with her "third time lucky" husband, Dan. Because of her stepson's behavioural issues and her own health concerns, she'd radically changed the family's diet. We met one frigid February weekday for lunch at a new restaurant with a gluten-free menu.

"It's good to see you," I said, as I hugged her.

"You too, it's been too long."

We had our choice of tables in the austere surroundings.

"I don't know how this kind of niche restaurant is going to make it way out here on International Avenue in a strip mall," I said.

"The rent is probably cheap."

"True. If the food is good, maybe they'll have a chance."

We quickly scanned the menu, made our choices, and ordered.

"So, how have you been feeling?" I asked.

"Pretty good. Watching my diet. I feel better if I stick to gluten-free grains and no dairy. I've pretty much cut out sugar too."

"Good for you. You've got more discipline than I do."

"I have to. If I don't, my IBS flares up. It's painful. And, menopause is throwing me for a loop. I'm doing some light therapy and energy work to help stay in balance and build up myself up. But, the most concerning thing right now," she said, as she pulled up her pant leg, "is this lump on my shin. It's growing and it hurts when I walk."

"Oooooh, what's up with that? Have you had it looked at?"

"I'm going for a biopsy next week. I'm not sure sticking a needle into it is a good idea but the doctor says he won't know how to proceed until he knows what he's dealing with."

"How do *you* want to proceed?" I asked, knowing she felt the same way about Allopathic medicine as I did—not too confident, and a practice we preferred to stay away from. Neither of us used pharmaceuticals if we could manage with natural products. We had both studied complementary modalities extensively and built our own businesses helping others with alternatives. Nicola tended more toward the spiritual and metaphysical aspects relating to health and I had assisted clients with their psycho-emotional healing and offered nutritional guidance.

"Honestly, I just don't know what to think right now. I'm kind of scared. The thing isn't going away with my efforts so … maybe it's time for drastic measures. I'll decide after I get the results and consult with the doctor."

"Fair enough. You don't have to decide right now. You'll let me know what happens, right?"

"For sure." We were silent for a moment. Then she changed the subject. "How are your plans coming along? Are you ready to go?"

"I'm freaking out a bit. I wake up sometimes in the morning because I can't breathe. Anxious I guess."

"To be expected, it's a big move."

"Yeah…huge. I was hoping to travel, use Buenos Aires as my home base, but I didn't get the tour guide job I thought I'd cinched. They probably decided I was too old. Just as well. I'd end up taking care of people all over again instead of just doing what I want."

"What do you want to do?"

"Dance, of course." I grinned. "Write, learn more Spanish, maybe teach English, travel around. I'll see what else when I get there."

Our food arrived. I'd ordered the mini sliders because they were just so darn cute—three miniature hamburgers on gluten-free buns dressed with cherry tomato slices. Nicola had a mixed-greens salad and we indulged in a shared order of yam fries.

"How are Amy and Amanda?" she asked between mouthfuls. "You saw them through their first Christmas without their dad? That's always the hardest. Are they okay with all the changes?"

"Hard to tell. They don't share a lot. They're both kind of depressed, of course. It'll take time. They say they're okay with me leaving, but who knows..."

"I'm sure they'll be fine. We were. They've got lots of family around for support."

"I know, but I still feel bad. They don't get along that great with their stepmom. I mean, she's okay, she's just...you know... going through her own stuff right now too."

"Of course. It was quite a shock for her. It's probably good for her to have the girls there with her."

"Plus, with her own two daughters, the house is full."

"Don't worry so much about them. Go and have an experience you'll never forget. You're showing them they can do it too at some point when they're ready to fly."

"I guess."

We picked at the remainder of the fries and reminisced about the past—a time when things seemed easier, more hopeful.

"You're lucky you've got Dan," I said wistfully. "He's crazy about you."

"I know. Who would have thought..."

"You're doing better than me for sure. Two husbands down and not another viable prospect in sight."

"Perhaps you'll meet a tall, dark and handsome tango dancer."

"One can dream…but seriously…I just need a break. I need to just focus on myself for a while. Figure out exactly what I want. Make better choices."

"Good idea."

We finished our meal, paid our bill, hugged each other like we meant it, wished each other well, and went our separate ways.

A couple weeks later, I received a voicemail from Nicola. The results of her biopsy were positive. She had osteosarcoma—bone cancer. It was aggressive. The doctor had elicited fear in her; he pressured her to begin chemotherapy and radiation as soon as possible in an effort to save her leg. Against her better judgment, Nicola succumbed. She said she would use complementary therapies to offset the side effects of the chemicals. It didn't seem fair. She was one of the most aware and health-conscious people I knew. I called her back to wish her well but there was no answer.

CHAPTER 4

Tango Tourists

Some dance to remember, some dance to forget.

Don Henley, *Hotel California*

The hum of conversation from the courtyard below my window eased me awake. I recognized a few words of Spanish, but mostly, the dialogue between the two women was a pleasant lull. After a fitful night on the airplane, I'd slept well.

I lay in bed and recalled the past 24 hours. *What have I done?* I'd left behind everything familiar. Panic about leaping into an unknown future had had me waking some mornings gasping for air. Now that I'd leapt, I was able to breathe again. I thought about what I wanted to do for a couple days before the rest of the tango crowd from Calgary arrived for our three-week tour. I looked forward to exploring the neighbourhood and getting my bearings.

I showered, dressed and descended the narrow staircase to the deserted kitchen. I had no groceries, so I went out into the *barrio* of Almagro in search of breakfast. A *café con leche* and some moist *medialunas* would hit the spot.

The beginning of autumn had taken the top off the heat in the southern hemisphere. Since I'd intended to do a lot of walking, I'd donned my Birkenstocks and bared my toes. German sandals pegged me as a foreigner. Broken sidewalks and cobblestone streets begged for safe and comfortable shoes, yet, most women wore heels. I saved mine for the dance floor.

Entering a quiet corner café, I plopped myself down by the window and checked the menu, then stumbled through my order in Spanish. I stared out the window at the activity on Avenida Rivadavia. Shopkeepers sprayed down the sidewalk in front of their establishments while pedestrians sidestepped the spray; drivers leaned on their horns as if the blast would part traffic for them; motorcycle couriers sped by, some with helmet in hand so they could talk on a cell phone. I celebrated my decision to come to this frenetic city. I loved Buenos Aires. Not because it was easy to love, but because it would never bore me.

After the sweet, moist mini croissants and a perfect cup of coffee, I hit the cement and walked until my hips hurt. Even if I closed my eyes, there was something about the smell of my surroundings that informed me I wasn't in "Kansas" anymore. I wasn't used to being immersed in car exhaust and the smoke from foreign cigarettes. I caught whiffs of unfamiliar perfumes and colognes as people passed by. The language sounded like music to my ears; I could only hum a few bars.

Some of my favourite places had disappeared in the past two years: the *locutorio* where I'd checked my email, the *heladeria* where I'd tried a different flavour of ice cream each evening. *Mmm, dulce de leche...* I looked forward to establishing new favourite places.

I ventured farther, into the *microcentro,* to look around. On the narrow Calle Suipacha, across from the historic tango venue, Confitería Ideal, I gazed longingly at the myriad of tango shoes in display cases: *Those heels are so high. Those sparkly ones are gorgeous. I should probably just get basic black. Oooh, what about those red ones...* I would be back several times before choosing new shoes. Several pairs. Then, I headed down Calle Florida, a wide pedestrian mall lined with a plethora of shops and services. At its other end, in the magnificent Galerías Pacífico shopping mall, I picked up a schedule for the month's dance classes at Escuela Argentino de Tango. True to its name, the *galería* had frescoes gracing its high, domed ceiling and an exhibition of contemporary art in an actual gallery space near the *escuela*. *I'm going to love this place.*

Pickings were limited at the small grocery store near Pilar's. Other than its tender, grass-fed beef, Argentina's not really known for its food. Since I was a health-conscious foodie, I would have to hunt for better places to shop: produce markets and health food stores. I needed more cheese choices and grainier bread. I purchased half a small roasted chicken, salad fixings, and a bottle of Malbec for my dinner. The next day's breakfast would be fruit and yogourt.

I chatted with a few of my housemates in the cozy courtyard of the *casa* while the warmth of the sun waned. I sipped my wine and enjoyed my meal, then read a few Spanish paragraphs about Nietzsche before turning in early. Loosening one's chains is exhausting.

After two nights at Pilar's, I took a taxi to Caseron Porteño in Palermo where I would join my friends, dancers from my hometown tango community. The organizers had arrived earlier but were staying a block away at a different *caseron*. The rest of the gang dribbled in throughout the day.

I'd timed my arrival in Buenos Aires to coincide with the tango tour; having familiar dancers to go to *milongas* with would help me ease into my new life. The fact that I had already been in Buenos Aires two days and not danced showed an unfortunate lack of dedication, but I wasn't brave enough to go to a *milonga* by myself. I envisioned an eventual lifestyle of dancing until dawn, returning to my apartment to journal about the day's events, donning earplugs and an eyeshade, and attempting to sleep through the day. An unlikely fantasy; my circadian rhythms balked at the thought of disruption.

Kyle and I had been acquaintances for a long time, then dated for about two years. I introduced him to tango and he was hooked. He'd wanted to take a tango tour to the Motherland and the timing was right for the two of us to explore the city and dance with a familiar partner before I ventured out on my own. This adventure would be our last "tango" together.

Kyle arrived mid-afternoon. He greeted me with a kiss as he wrapped his arms around me. I could tell he was already uncomfortable with the heat.

"How was your flight?" I asked.

"It was pretty hard on my back. I'm looking forward to just lying down for a quick nap. Join me? You can tell me about the past couple days."

He checked in at the back office while I waited in the garden. The *caseron* was next to a schoolyard, separated by a high, heavily-vined cement wall, and the children had just returned after their three-month summer break. It was noisy.

Our room was next to the main door, which clanged each time someone came or went. Whispers echoed in the hallway. Pedestrians walked past our necessarily-open window. Cars whizzed by with honking horns. An unpleasant musty smell emanated from our windowless bathroom. Too much humidity. Easing in was not going to be easy.

After dinner, the group gathered in the dance studio at the back of the garden to practice. Maya, one of our favourite teachers who had been to Calgary, was invited to oversee our practice and prepare us for the Buenos Aires' *milongas*. Afterward, we went to Salón Canning's Milonga Parakultural. Canning was located on Avenida Scalabrini Ortiz in Palermo, which used to be Canning Street, hence the moniker. It seemed we'd arrived at the end of the "afternoon" *milonga* and had a half hour before the evening *milonga* started. We waited.

A funky little "store" with all kinds of tango paraphernalia spilled out of the men's washroom and into the corridor. Recently refurbished, the main room had a polished wooden floor overseen by a huge mural that depicted a room full of *tangueros*. A new coat of paint covered what must have been years of smoke damage to the walls. Since the last time I'd been to this venue, Buenos Aires had changed its public smoking by-laws. My "virgin" lungs were pleased that they wouldn't have to endure a smokey haze whenever I went out.

Although I loved the dance, I thought tango music was more of an acquired taste, kind of like beer. I had only ever heard recordings and referred to the oldies as "scratchy" tango music. Maybe it would grow on me. Maybe I would like it better when I heard real instruments played by real musicians in real time. I looked forward to that.

We watched the *milongueros* dance, hoping to observe some of the proper etiquette before we got out onto the floor. Even though the temperature outside was near thirty degrees Celsius, many of the local men wore suits. The women were costumed in an array of colourful dresses. Their footwork, highlighted by stunning shoes, was mesmerizing. Everyone looked elegant and masterful, following the line of dance, and never bumping into each other even as the floor filled.

Once the floor filled, men and women were no longer able to perform the *cabeceo* ritual that tango etiquette called for because they were sitting on opposite sides of the room, unless they'd come with friends as we had. During the short *cortina* between *tandas,* women would stare (the *mirada*) at the men they wanted to dance with. If gazes met, men would nod (the *cabeceo)* and rise to join the woman on the dance floor. With this silent invitation, men didn't risk public rejection and women chose only the men they wanted to dance with. This was something our group hadn't yet practiced in our own community. It would take us a while to get warmed up to the idea if we wanted to dance with anyone outside of our group.

Traditional tango on a crowded floor wouldn't allow for the excessive movements our dancers were used to performing on the spacious Canadian dance floors. Our leaders were going to have to learn to take smaller steps to deftly navigate their way through dense dance traffic.

Kyle and I had never danced particularly well together. One would think we were well-suited: both tall and slim; but that wasn't the body type that allowed for nestling into a comfortable *milonguero* embrace. Arching to meet his chest hurt my lower back. He was graceful, led well, and followed the rules, but he was hard to get close to. Our tour leader Ricardo, on the other hand, was not only a superb dancer, but his barrel chest made it easy to cuddle into his embrace. He was a pleasure to dance with.

Kyle and I stayed for a few *tandas* and, not used to late-night starts, returned to the *caseron* while the majority of the group stayed. Kyle would only be in Buenos Aires a short time and we both wanted to enjoy our days and take in the sights.

The next day, we dawdled over breakfast and chatted with the other guests. Then, we decided to go to the stunning Planetario Galileo Galilei. Kyle was a bit of a science geek. We took a taxi to Parque Tres de Febrero to the planetarium. We walked through, looking at the displays, but didn't want to watch a star show inside on such a beautiful day. Instead, we strolled around the lake and through the park.

That evening, the group headed to Club Gricel, a moderately-sized salon in *barrio* San Cristóbal, with an exquisite floor and a garish neon sign above the bar at the back. We arrived early enough to participate in the class before the *milonga*. Miguel Angel Pla arrived to assist one of his student teachers with her class. He had been to Calgary, so some of us knew him. A retired doctor, Pla had taken up tango late in life and went on to become an award-winning dancer, and later, a master teacher of the salon style. He was a nice man and we had enjoyed learning from his expertise.

On Sunday evening, we only had to walk a block and across the bridge to La Milonguita. A small-neighbourhood *milonga*, it was more to my liking. For a few pesos, we were entertained by Sexteto Milonguero. The musicians were young and energetic, long-haired, and informally dressed in jeans and t-shirts. They made traditional music sound contemporary. The lead singer was tall, dark and passionate, with a smile that didn't stop. I thought of him as the Mick Jagger of tango with a little Benicio del Toro thrown in for the Che effect. The passion of the musicians stirred the passion of the dancers with the vibration of instrument and voice. Everyone looked like they were having fun, on stage and off. What a difference it made to tango to live music. I knew then that I could grow to appreciate the complexity of tango music. And to love it.

Over the two weeks, the members of our group engaged in the usual tourist activities, took classes at various schools and venues, and had private lessons in the back studio of the *caseron*. We went to a tango show next door to the Museo del Jamon—the Museum of Ham. Tango shows for tourists are not at all like the tango danced in *milongas*. Traditionally, Argentine tango is an intimate social dance that expresses music full of sadness. The floors are crowded, the embrace is close and the steps are small. It's not like the gymnastic versions shown on television competitions for entertainment or the "tango for export" shows performed at tourist venues. The performance we saw in Puerto Madero was an exhibitionist spectacle—a mediocre "prostitution" of tango. I guess I was already a tango snob.

Kyle and I tolerated each other well. We were restrained, pleasant and accommodating—which was part of the reason we would never have been able to sustain a long-term relationship—not the kind I wanted. I wanted something deeper and more honest.

He wanted to take a day trip to Uruguay. I wanted to save that trip for when I needed it—when my 90-day visa neared expiration and I'd have to leave, and re-enter, Argentina. But, Kyle's time was short and I wanted him to enjoy his holiday, so I agreed to go.

We took the Buquebus across the Rio de la Plata, the second-widest river in the world, to Colonia, a sleepy town that wakes up to tourists. We wandered the cobblestone streets of the small historic area and admired the integration of Spanish and Portuguese influences; the Spanish encouraged street drainage down the middle of the street and the Portuguese encouraged it down the sides. We ascended the lighthouse tower and we took a short bus tour past the bullring that got little use before it was shut down due to the ban on bullfights. Up the highway we went to the one-time Guinness Book record holder for the largest collection of pencils. As one's interest in pencils must assuredly wane, the owner of the "museum" also had enormous collections of key tags and pop cans and other assorted…junk, displayed in numerous cabinets against the walls. It ended up being an interesting trip and we had a good day.

The next day, Kyle came with me to view the apartment I would rent for six months as of the middle of May. It was a tango fantasy come true: right on Corrientes Street in the retail area of Once. The owner, Ray, seemed quite pleasant but spoke almost no English. I would have to work out the details with his brother, a realtor, whose office was just up the street. The recently-renovated apartment was small and spartan, but equipped with everything I would need, except a couch in the living room.

Then we headed to the Recoleta Cemetery to pay obligatory homage to Eva Peron's tomb and stroll around the intriguing necropolis. The gated cemetery was originally a garden attached to the still-standing church and convent during the 1700s. All the vaults were above ground and laid out like a labyrinth of city blocks. Housing the rich and famous, mausoleums were adorned with marble statues in a variety of classic architectural styles. It was like a museum—full of ghosts and stories. I was fascinated by the locks that secured the tombs, especially those covered in cobwebs, and took photos of select details: wrought-iron designs, reflections, shadows, rust and webs.

"Do you think they're trying to keep looters out, or are they locking in the dead so they don't escape?" I asked Kyle, tongue in cheek.

"I'm sure the families are worried about vandalism and theft," was his practical reply. "But, you sure have a good eye for detail," he said, as he looked through my photos.

"Thanks. This place inspires me, there's so much to see. I'll have to come back."

La Catedral *milonga* was held in a building built before 1900 in the Almagro *barrio*, just a few blocks from Pilar's. It was originally used as a grain silo and then a manufacturing plant for dairy products; it was finally recovered as a cultural site by the city. I didn't see anything worth saving as far as architecture, but its history was interesting. The wide, worn wooden staircase led up to the entrance of a room famous for its grunge factor. Inside, the 12-metre-high walls were cluttered with *objetos de arte*—if you believe one man's junk is another man's treasure. It was like a flea market. The tables and chairs were mismatched and in disrepair. The dance floor looked like a danger zone: There were holes in the worn planks, and although it wasn't the kind of venue a woman should wear heels to anyway, she'd have to take extra care not to get them caught if she did. It's hard to surrender when you're being vigilant. There was a separate room for smoking and quieter conversation. I was intrigued by the "grittiness" of the venue, but the rest of our group had no interest in staying to dance in that kind of atmosphere. I would have to come back another time with liberal-minded dancers.

On the last Saturday night before Kyle's departure, our small group trekked far from the central tango scene to the suburb of Villa Urquiza. La Milonga del Mundo started in the 1940s in a huge basketball court of a sports club. Sunderland, as it's referred to, had fluorescent lighting on the high ceiling and painted lines on the linoleum floor. Folding tables and stacking chairs completed the lack of ambience. With that, and little publicity, Sunderland miraculously survived as one of the most famous *milonga* locations. Eager Canadians, we were among the first to arrive for the 10:30 *milonga* and ordered a late dinner. The food was basic, and as bad as the ambience.

By midnight, the gym was packed with high-calibre dancers of all ages. The guidebook suggested that dancers at Sunderland adhere to the strict *codigos* of authentic *milongas*, which seemed antithetical to being in a gymnasium unconducive to using the *cabeceo*. Most couples danced in close embrace but the overall style seemed pretty flexible. In defiance of *codigos*, Miguel Angel Pla, who had reconnected with us the previous week at Club Gricel, walked over to our table and held out his hand to me.

Are you kidding?

It was difficult to maintain composure as I fell into his embrace and closed my eyes. He was easy on me—treated me gently while we danced to up-beat *milonga* music.

"How long will you be in Buenos Aires?" he asked when the music stopped.

"I plan to be here about eighteen months," I replied.

"Ah, good. That should be enough time."

I took his comment as a polite way of suggesting I could benefit from a lot of practice.

CHAPTER 5

House of Grief

Tango is the only dance in the world not intended to express joy.
Danced properly, it should be passionate yet loveless as a one-night stand.

Miranda France, *Bad Times in Buenos Aires*

After Kyle and the rest of the Calgarians went home, I returned to Pilar's. It would be six weeks before I could move into my apartment. It was time for me to settle in and establish a routine. I had a larger room at the front of the *casa*, overlooking the street. The clip clop of horses' hooves and wooden wheels of the *cartoneros'* wagons initiated my morning struggle. I argued with myself about what I wanted and what I *should* do. Now that I was left on my own without a solid plan, my feelings started to surface. The whisper of desire was difficult to hear from under the heavy blanket of grief. I had trouble caring. Maybe if grief were paid enough attention, it would retreat satisfied and allow the voice of desire to have its turn. I changed my mind so many times, skeptical that answers would appear at just the right moment.

I knew I *should* start going to *milongas* by myself, but it felt like too much of an effort. I was a chicken. I had promised myself I would go to early classes but, exhausted by my internal warfare, I succumbed to a few more moments of sweet slumber instead. If making friends with grief was all I could manage to accomplish for now, it would have to be enough.

Several housemates came and went during my stay. Aja was a beautiful thirty-something daughter of a British rock star from the 70s. She was used to Seattle's clean air, healthy food, and yoga, but she deteriorated during her visit. Her husband had left her for another woman. They'd met dancing tango in Buenos Aires four years earlier, so she was back to visit the scene of the crime. She threw herself into tango—preferring classes and *practicas* to *milongas*. When she did go to a *milonga*, the men hovered around her, eager for a chance to pounce. I admired her rejection of "obligatory" high heels for more-comfortable flat shoes. But she seemed to be pushing herself and not enjoying it.

Mary, another guest, was supposed to come to Buenos Aires with her boyfriend. But the day after she'd booked their trip, they broke up. Like me, she was a massage therapist looking for a new direction. But she was only staying nine days and didn't feel much like dancing. Even so, she joined me in the pursuit of the perfect shoes.

One afternoon, Mary and I found ourselves in the middle of a demonstration against the increase in taxes on the export of soy products while on our way to the shoe store. Although Argentina is the world's third largest producer of soy, most of it is exported. Wealthy landowners sent busloads of paid demonstrators into the city; thousands marched, banged pots, carried banners and blocked traffic. Protests on the highways outside the city kept food products from getting to the supermarket shelves. Argentines always seemed to be protesting but, I was told, it was unusual to see a protest of this duration and magnitude.

We'd crossed a main street downtown, dodging protesters, to get to one of the stores across from Confitería Ideal. In addition to the commotion, the lingering haze and overcast sky facilitated an early "twilight" and many stores were closing early. The steel gate of the shoe store was halfway down so we ducked under; the shopgirl said she was waiting for her boss to call back and tell her it was okay to close. Her fear appeared to increase as the demonstrators got louder. She told us we should run. We hadn't been afraid until then. Fortunately, within a few moments, the wind picked up and a storm blew in, bringing rain, and the protesters dispersed. Mary and I made it home wet, but safe.

Alice, an older woman in our *casa*, was out dancing almost every night of her six-week stay. "I do not like to look at the men," she said with a Parisian accent. So, without the *mirada* part of the *cabeceo* ritual, she waited for men to come to her. She didn't relish returning to Paris where, she said, "The dancing is not so great." As a Calgarian, I couldn't imagine that to be true. But we were in the Motherland of Tango, so I guess it's all a matter of perspective.

Pepe's wife left him after both their sons died five years ago. He moved to Buenos Aires from Cuba. He soothed his sorrow dancing salsa. What else could he do?

These were the people who lived in my *casa*. We were all grieving something.

Ж

Buenos Aires has one of the highest ratios of therapists to inhabitants in the world—on par with New York. I don't know what that says about a population. Either citizens are highly self-reflective or they're really messed up. I thought it would be a good idea to have someone "witness" my journey and give me unbiased feedback. I searched for a local therapist who was fluent in English. I picked through the expat sites and the local English newspaper and narrowed it down to three. The first kept looking out the window at the school across the street. She seemed agitated. She explained, in passable English, that her daughter went to school there, but she didn't explain why she was distracted. Call me a narcissist but...I didn't want to talk to someone who couldn't keep her attention on me—when I was paying her to do just that.

I attended a lecture about relationships that my second candidate was presenting. She appeared to be quite full of herself and I thought she subtly belittled the men in the audience. I didn't like that kind of "feminism." Strike two.

I settled on Carlotta. I liked her right away. She had lived in the United States, so understood what it was like to be an expat and then a repatriate, and her English was excellent. Her office was near the cemetery.

Even though it was a cold, cloudy, and windy day, I'd chosen to walk to the Recoleta Cemetery before my appointment to get some exercise and blow off steam. The rain was welcome and refreshing. The *aires* hadn't been so *buenos* lately as the smoke drifted in from the crops burning for rotation since the soy tax increase. A haze settled on the city and caused havoc with residents' allergies, but it softened the light, making it ideal for shooting photos. As I walked, the wind kept lifting the umbrella's skirt, exposing its fragile bones.

Where is he when you need him? Oh ya,... he's dead. Fucker. Just when you think it's okay to rely on somebody, they go and die. Irresponsible father—gone in a flash without goodbye. Fucking dead.

The drizzle stopped just in time for me to pull out my camera and get a few interesting shots. I typically stayed away from cemeteries but, being like an art gallery, this one had caught my attention. Maybe there was something there for me. I found beauty in the juxtaposition of twisted iron and smooth glass, the interplay of shadow and light, and the way interiors were revealed and while neighbouring exteriors were reflected at the same time. I didn't know what I would do with the images; but it was something for me to focus on. I could figure the rest out later; perhaps a bigger project would present itself. In the process, I hoped to assuage my grief.

A couple, carved in stone, sat up high on the foundation of their family tomb: he sat in a chair facing one direction and only a bust of her faced the other. I overheard a tour guide tell her group that the couple were thought to still be arguing in the afterlife. I wondered if, without material distractions and petty grievances, there could be forgiveness between them. Maybe in the evening, after the cemetery closed, the light faded and the chatter diminished, their eternal bodies finally lay together at peace with each other. I wondered if I would find peace with my ex now that he was gone.

I arrived at my therapist's office and she buzzed me in. It was a comfortable-looking shared apartment office. I sat across from her at her desk. "What can I do for you," she asked.

I revealed enough of my backstory so Carlotta could understand why I was in Buenos Aires and where my head was at. I told her I had just come from the cemetery. "It's like a little oasis in the city, so peaceful," I said. "I enjoy discovering unusual aspects of beauty with my camera."

"Maybe this will be a way to heal your grief," she said.

"Maybe." I looked down at my hands in my lap. "You'd think dancing would help."

"Doesn't it?"

"Well, the actual act of dancing does make me feel better. It's just...there's so much else tied up with it that's distressing."

"Like what?"

"Finding the motivation to go out and potentially not even dance... I can't deal with that. Dancing with creepy guys, watching other dancers enjoy themselves, I feel kind of insecure and left out."

"Have you made any friends here?"

"Sure. But they come and go, or they don't dance, or we just don't connect."

"What about Argentine men? Do you like Argentine men?"

"Well, most of the ones I've seen on the dance floor are old, short and unattractive…although,…I have seen some handsome, tall *porteños*. But, so what? It's hard enough to have a relationship with a man who comes from my own culture and speaks the same language, never mind the extra barriers. Besides, I've heard most of them are pretty arrogant and misogynist."

Carlotta smiled. "They're not all like that."

"I suppose not. But I've kinda decided I'm off men right now anyway, I'm not seriously looking. I just want to dance."

"That's probably wise. You have a lot going on right now. It sounds like you're taking some good actions toward healing your grief. It takes time. It will sort itself out."

CHAPTER 6
Maintaining Balance

What I am looking for is not out there. It is in me.

Helen Keller

In the Centro Región Leonesa on Humberto Primo was the Milonga de los Consagrados; it started late on Saturday afternoons and went into the early evening. I ascended the majestic marble staircase. A heavy red velvet curtain separated the lobby and washrooms from the tables and dance floor.

I'd connected with Cherie through a *tanguera* back home, and met her when Don and I had visited before. After her husband died, Cherie took off to discover the world of dance and eventually landed in Buenos Aires. She hosted a table each week with her partner, Ruben, for their friends and students. As a solo newcomer, I would have been assigned a seat somewhere at the back of the women's side of the room. But, I was fortunate to be welcome at Cherie's table anytime. I made a beeline for her mixed-gender table on the men's side of the room. I felt comforted to know a few people, even if only a little.

"Maraya, it's good to see you again," Cherie said as she rose to hug me.

"You too. Thank you for letting me join you at your table. I've been nervous to go out to *milongas* on my own."

"Hola, Maraya, bienvenidos." Ruben greeted me with an obligatory *beso* on my cheek. *"Querés champagne?"* he asked as he lifted the bottle and poured bubbly into a glass without waiting for my response.

"Sure, *gracias,*" I replied and took the glass.

"How have you been? You've been in B.A. for a few weeks already, right? Have you been dancing?" asked Cherie, trying to get a quick update before she was whisked off again to dance.

"I'm good. Yeah, we went to a few *milongas* while the group was here. I've been lucky to ease in and have a few familiar partners to dance with. Now I have to get brave and see if I can keep up with strangers…assuming I'll eventually get asked to dance."

"Oh, don't worry, you'll be fine."

Cherie explained the *cabeceo* to me. It was good to get a refresher from an expert. Once the floor fills, eye contact across it is obstructed. That's when the less desirable dancers make a move to try to charm unsuspecting female tourists onto the floor.

Cherie told me if I wanted to dance I would have to make eye contact. "He's a good dancer," she said as she pointed. "Him too."

I looked at them and wondered why the hell I would want to dance with either of them. The thought of pressing my chest against a geriatric stranger, my temple against his sweaty brow, his cologne and his previous partners' make-up and perfume mingling with mine, while he clutched me and restricted my movement. I didn't want to dance a bad tango to music I didn't like with a man I didn't know. *Why, exactly, am I here?* I preferred to just watch the dancers, admire the shoes, and talk to my friends.

But, someone snuck up behind me and I was secretly pleased to be asked. I didn't want to go a whole evening without dancing. He was much older than me and almost as tall. Since I didn't choose, I couldn't complain. We faced each other on the floor, smiled, and exchanged niceties in Spanish. We embraced and I closed my eyes, nervous, but offering my trust. We moved. I didn't always do what he wanted me to do; since it was our first time together we didn't communicate well. Still, he complimented my ability to dance after the first song. I smiled and said, *"Gracias,"* but I didn't believe him. I felt like a fool, a beginner, a klutz. *This is tango hell.*

The dance floor was so crowded that the next move was either going to hurt me or someone else. Heels, usually my own, scraped across the delicate skin on the top of my feet. Bodies brushed against unknown bodies, unable to do little more than sway. After three songs, we'd made it all the way around the dance floor; I was quick to say thank you and sit down again in the safe harbour of friends. I took a big gulp of champagne.

I felt like everyone was looking, judging, and recording unfamiliar faces: Where they were from, what they wore, where they sat, whom they sat with, danced with, and left with. I wasn't paranoid.

"Es asi," Cherie concurred. She'd been here long enough to know.

I got a good look across to the other side of the floor before it filled up again. *The women look like a row of sitting ducks, make-up over surgery, provocative clothing, and the men are mostly old, short, and sweaty. I hate tango music. What the hell am I doing here? How absurd to get dressed up and squirm around like a can of live sardines. What was I thinking?*

I sensed a tremor in the foundation of my future in Buenos Aires. My preparations, my plans, my hopes and dreams, began to crumble under the weight of the reality that I already didn't like the tango scene: Pressed breasts and chests, tangled legs, gyrating on an impossibly crowded dance floor. There was a falsity about the search for intimacy in the embrace of a stranger. There was a moment sought, no matter how brief, when the music, the movement, would hopefully sweep one away from the harsh world toward Nirvana. Like that one kiss Rumi described—you wait the whole of your life for that one tango.

Is it worth the effort?

The craziness came over me like a tsunami. Maybe I'd reached my limit by playing nice with Kyle; maybe I was second-guessing my choice to run away from home. I'd read that expats cycled through emotions as they settled in; maybe this was to be expected. I was supposed to be having fun but I felt like bursting into tears and there was no privacy. Maybe I could have mentioned it to Cherie, she'd have probably understood, but she was busy dancing and hosting. *Should I just leave? Should I run to the bathroom and hide?* Someone would undoubtedly question the pained expression on my face and I did not have a sensical answer. I would have to claim menopause.

Just get your shit together, suck it up. Save it for your therapy session.

Oh...okay.... Nervous breakdown averted. I did what I'm best at: *Just keep on keeping on.*

I'd gotten over my first major hurdle; I'd gone to a *milonga* without a partner. But, I preferred to take a class; I didn't have to dress up for a class; I was guaranteed to dance in a class; and I would get to change partners and meet people from all over the world. Maybe I'd meet people to go to *milongas* with. I would likely speak to someone in English, who wouldn't feed me *chamuyo* (flirtatious bullshit), and who had a mind open enough to think he might also learn something. The atmosphere was infinitely more relaxed in a class.

In Aurora's technique class today at the Escuela Argentino de Tango, many of us were fighting to maintain balance. I tried not to topple. Once it became easy in flat shoes, we put on heels and I wobbled anew. I couldn't even walk with grace. Our *maestra* instructed, "Ladies, there is no need to have your arms spread out as if you're about to grasp something. Balance is not somewhere "out there"; balance is within. It rises up from your center, straight up the invisible silver cord to the top of your head where it connects you to the sky, and thus creates your alignment."

Later, she told me I was placing too much weight onto my partner. "Stop leaning on him," she said. "You must learn to maintain your own balance and to dance alone. Then, dance with a man but not *on* him."

Good advice. The metaphor was not lost on me.

CHAPTER 7

Re-establishing a Sense of Direction

"Would you tell me, please, which way I ought to go from here?"
"That depends a good deal on where you want to get to," said the Cat.
"I don't much care where——" said Alice.
"Then it doesn't matter which way you go," said the Cat.
"——as long as I get SOMEWHERE," Alice added as an explanation.
"Oh, you're sure to do that," said the Cat, "if you only walk long enough."

Lewis Carroll, *Alice's Adventures in Wonderland*

I settled in for a six-month duration in my own apartment on Corrientes—the main artery into the heart of the city. I felt like I'd finally landed. I was starting to establish a groove and rhythm for myself. Just having my own apartment was, in itself, a new adventure. Since I was on the seventh floor at the back of the building, I wasn't affected by the traffic noises from Corrientes.

I decided to heed Carlotta's advice and make an effort to meet more new people. Maybe I would find a dance partner I could go to classes and *milongas* with. A partner would help me get out more and onto the dance floor. Even meeting people who didn't dance would get me out and about, enjoying myself.

Right next door was a tango studio in an old house where yoga classes were offered. I thought I'd ease my way into the studio by attending the yoga classes, designed specifically for tango dancers. Not entirely familiar with yoga, especially in Spanish, I did my best to follow what Maxi, the handsome young yogi, was doing. After classes, I often ate lunch on the patio with some of the regulars. Most of the teachers and many of the participants were much younger than me and, as much as I liked them, I felt like an outsider.

I found a Spanish school only four blocks away and enrolled in group classes for a month of half days. Again, most were younger but we had a fun time getting to know each other. None of them danced tango.

I looked for opportunities to teach English and dropped off a few resumes, but the pay, weighed against the time to get to some of those places, didn't seem worth the effort, especially if I had to take a cab. I soon gave up on the idea of teaching English.

I found a Newcomers' group for English expats and attended a meeting, then signed up for some of their activities. It was a nice group of people, mostly older and mostly retired Americans. I met Linda at one of the dinners. She'd left her New York home about four years previous. Her husband had died three years before that—and good riddance to him—he'd been abusive. Linda had been a counselling psychologist and had written a book related to her career. I told her I was interested in starting an English writers' group and she thought it was a great idea. She was planning to write a second book and would appreciate the support of like-minded people. We agreed to meet for lunch the following week to discuss the details.

Ж

Daylight Savings Time messed with my head. When I first arrived in Buenos Aires there was a five-hour time difference between it and Calgary. A week later, there was a four-hour difference. Another week later, there was only a three-hour difference. Alberta had "sprung forward" and Argentina had "fallen back," minimizing the gap between them. But, even after a couple months, I still felt like I was three hours behind. I struggled with equilibrium and continued to experience vertigo as my brain attempted to catch up with my body. With the churning in my head, I strove to find stillness in the eye of the tornado of fifteen million inhabitants.

For the directionally challenged, Buenos Aires can be disorienting. Every day I was literally (and metaphorically) faced with figuring out where I was, where I was going, and how to get there. Although the sun still made its daily appearance in the east, it traversed the northern sky, not the southern like I was used to, before it set in the west. I found this disconcerting. If the sun was shining, as it usually was, I could discern my location by spotting the glow between buildings in the dense concrete downtown core. But, most of the time I was in shadows, carefully watching where I placed my feet so as not to twist an ankle on broken sidewalk blocks or step in dog shit.

I'd always had pretty good spatial sense, and my ability to read a map had come in handy in the past. But tourist maps of *el centro de* Buenos Aires were all printed with north situated somewhere right to lower right with west-southwest situated at the top. The maps showed the coastline of *el Río Tigre* at the bottom of the page instead of at the right—the eastern boundary of the city. Maybe they thought it was more visually appealing to underscore the city with the river along the bottom of the map.

I realized the map was offset from the norm (my norm) several weeks after I'd arrived. And, believing that north is always at the top of a map, I had imprinted inaccurate information upon my brain's positioning database. It was no wonder I travelled in the wrong direction several times before I found my way.

I had to purchase reading glasses and stand under streetlights to make sense of where I was, and my map became so worn at the folds it was falling apart.

If I go right when I get off the subte, and up the stairs, then I go right when I reach the street. If I go left when I get off the subte, then I go left when I hit the street.

I had to remember something similar at each station. Once out of the depths and onto the street, I had to walk a block to the corner, which often had no street sign, past that and proceed down another block to the next corner, which *may* have a street sign, before I walked back the two blocks and headed off in a different direction to try again. Good thing there are only four directions.

Eventually I had a weekly routine, with a regular transit pattern I could remember, and I didn't get lost quite so often. It usually took me longer to get somewhere than it should—unless I took a cab. But that felt like cheating; I would never take a taxi in Calgary. I liked to walk; it was good exercise.

Both major Canadian cities I've lived in numbered downtown streets consecutively, so there's little question what the next street would be—in any direction. No need for a map. But even though Buenos Aires was, more or less, built on a grid, where straight streets intersect straight streets, Avenida Alicia Moreau de Justo becomes Avenida Antartida Argentina when it intersects Avenida Cordoba at about a five-degree change in angle. That's only one example. Name changes at intersections indicated different political parties in office, different allegiances, and the need to honour someone different. Some of those names are ridiculously long for a street and simply didn't make their way onto my tiny map.

Buenos Aires not only professes to be home to the longest avenue in the world, but also the widest. Both these claims can be refuted. Avenida Nueve de Julio marks Argentina's independence from Spain in 1816. It is 300 feet wide with seven one-way lanes in each direction. There is a wide center median and each set of lanes is flanked by another two lanes—Cerrito southbound and Carlos Pellegrini northbound—also separated by wide medians. A pedestrian could safely get across half the width in one light. At the intersection of Nueve de Julio and Av. Corrientes, stands *el Obelisco*, the 67.5-meter high concrete symbol of the patriarchy—much like the one in Washington, D.C.

I made arrangements online to meet with an expat group at an art gallery on Sunday. The gallery was located on Sarmiento—which was the name of the street behind my apartment building. I decided to walk the several blocks through the deserted streets of the usually hopping shopping district of Once, searching for the address...that just wasn't there. *I don't understand.* I hailed a cab to bail me out.

I hopped into the back. "I am *so* late. Do you know where La Rural is on Sarmiento?"

"Por supuesto!" he replied

"But...*this* is Sarmiento, isn't it?"

"This is Sarmiento *Street.* La Rural is on Sarmiento *Avenue.*"

Oh...who knew.... I asked him to take me there.

All my life I'd thought streets in the core of a city aligned north to south and avenues went west to east. In Buenos Aires (and apparently other places too) streets are narrower, most of them uni-directional, and avenues are wide main thoroughfares with traffic in both directions.

La Rural was huge, and not an art gallery. More like an exhibition hall for hosting trade shows and events. It had been transformed into an over-sized gallery space of Latin American art. By the time I'd arrived, my group had dissipated into the crowd. With no cell phone, and no idea what any of them looked like, I wandered the exhibits alone and in awe—appreciating the art. As I contemplated the paintings, and my confusion subsided, I acknowledged how both art and travel expand us—if we let them. Everything I'd ever learned was at risk of being contradicted, discarded and replaced with something new. I'd picked the perfect place to discover a new direction.

CHAPTER 8

Blank Canvas

There are far better things ahead ...

C. S. Lewis

After my massage, Christina, my *masajista*, quietly led me to the hydrotherapy room. I sat my skinny naked body down in a plastic chair, facing an eight-by-eight-foot empty space—with a white-tiled wall and grey floor, older than me and riddled with cracks. The metal, dinner-plate-sized showerhead above me began pounding out a cool and uncomfortable spray. Behind the plastic curtain at my back, Christina adjusted levers and dials, to control temperature and pressure, on her console like the little man in *The Wizard of Oz*. I squirmed around in the chair to surrender every muscle of my back to the force while imagining myself a vulnerable prisoner alone in a water chamber being cleansed of the sin of my existence. These and other images tortured me as I neared a sort of death of the past fifty years on this pivotal birthday. Then, I focused ahead on the blank white wall of possibility.

I turned on Skype when I got back to my apartment at the end of the day. It wasn't long before I got a call from Amanda.

"Hi Mommy! Happy Birthday!"

"Thank you, honey."

"What did you do today?"

"I treated myself to a spa day at one of the hotels then coffee and cake at Café Tortoni."

"Nice. What did you get—a mani? Pedi? Massage?"

"Just a pedicure, a massage and some water treatments that were kind of weird. How are you? What did you do today?"

"I'm good. Worked early then had an afternoon class. Just studying for a test now."

"How's Amy? What's she up to?"

"Okay. She's at work. She said to say 'Happy Birthday' and she misses you."

"Tell her 'thanks.' I miss you guys too. I'm glad you called." I looked at my beautiful daughter and felt a pang of guilt and sadness. I missed my girls. I felt torn anew by wanting to be there for them and wanting to be here for me. *No tears.*

"Hey," I said, "I've been thinking, I promised you both that if you took Spanish in high school, I would treat you to a trip to a Spanish-speaking country, but I haven't been able to make good on that promise until now. I have my own apartment, and you both have your inheritance. I can contribute to your airfare. What do you think? Do you want to come for a visit?"

"Hmm, maybe…when were you thinking?"

"Well, when you can. Maybe August? Before school starts?"

"For how long?"

"Two weeks? It's a long way, expensive flight. No point coming for less time."

"That could probably work for me. I'd have to talk to Amy. What would we do there?"

Visiting with Mom must not have been enough of a draw. I'd have to figure out ways to keep them entertained and happy. "I know it's not exactly what you had in mind for a holiday, but I'd like to see you girls. You might never come this far if I weren't here. It might be interesting for you. We'll just hang out, go sightseeing, go shopping, meet my friends. Whatever you want."

"You have friends? Didn't you go out with your friends today?"

"No, you know I didn't want to make a big deal of my birthday. Yeah, I have some new friends. I've met a few people that I have things in common with. It takes time you know...to build a friendship. But, it's coming. I'm forcing myself to go out."

"What have you been doing?"

"Taking tango classes, going to a few *milongas*, going to newcomers' and expats' events. Spanish classes. I even started going to a therapist."

"What? Why? What's wrong?"

"Well, you know, it hasn't been an easy time for me either— lots of changes. It seems to be the thing to do here. It's way cheaper than seeing a therapist at home. I figured it'd be good to have someone give me some support and feedback."

"She speaks good English?"

"Yup. She used to live in the States. So, she understands the expat life."

"That sounds smart. Maybe I should do that. I'm just too busy."

"How are you doing, honey?"

"Okay. I guess.... I still really miss Dad. I get pretty depressed sometimes. But I just stay busy."

"How's Amy?"

"You know Amy. She doesn't talk much. I think she's really sad. Mostly she keeps it to herself. Sometimes we talk about Dad. She even cried once."

"Oh, good. That's a big step for her. She's lucky to have you there, you're a good sister. It gets better, I promise."

"Thanks, Mom.

She brushed away her tears and we just looked at each other for a moment. I wished I could have hugged her. *Damn.* There were so many times I hadn't been there for her when I should've been.

She was quick to shift the moment, albeit, not to anything happier. "Have you talked to Nicki lately? How's she doing?"

"Yeah. It's not good."

"What?"

"The chemo killed the cancer and another lump grew right beside the old location. She's pretty upset that she let them do a biopsy in the first place."

"Why? Didn't they have to? What's that got to do with it?"

"Well, when you puncture an encapsulated area you risk cells escaping into the rest of the body. It's called metastasizing."

"Is that what happened to Nicki?"

"Possibly. Probably. They can't say for sure. They want to amputate her leg below the knee to stop the potential spread."

"No way! That's crazy!"

"I can't believe it either. Makes no sense. But, I guess it's better than the alternative."

"I thought she was taking good care of herself."

"Apparently, cancer doesn't care."

"I know, right."

"So, this is all depressing. Anything good happening?"

"School is good—I like my classes. After my diploma I think I'll probably go to university and get my Social Work degree."

"Good idea."

"There's a guy in one of my classes I like. But, nothing's happened yet."

"Well, you can stay focused on your career. There will be lots of time for boys later."

"Yeah. What's next for you, Mom? What are your plans? Any trips?"

"Since I just went to Mendoza for a weekend, I have no other trips planned right now. But, in addition to more of what I already mentioned—kind of my regular schedule of stuff—I've decided to start a writers' group."

"That sounds cool."

"Yeah, I've met a few writers and I'm sure there are many more here. I'll advertise on Craigslist and hold weekly meetings—just to network and write and critique each other's work. Also, I've decided I need a dance partner. I'll have to get more assertive about finding one—just so I can get out more. I don't like going out at night by myself."

"Makes sense. Well, good luck with all that. Sounds like you have a good plan and lots to do."

"Yup, gotta stay busy. So, anyway, why don't you two plan a trip here—should be fun to focus on. Check your schedules, do a little research and find out what you want to see. I'll look into flights. It'll be good to spend some time together."

"Yeah, Mom, okay. I'll figure it out with my school and work and I'll get Amy to do the same."

"Good. I'm really glad you called. Best birthday present all day. Give Amy a big hug for me. I love you guys. Mwaaah! Big kiss.

"Same to you, Mom, love you. See ya!"

I shut down my laptop and had a little cry.

CHAPTER 9

Answering the Call

From: tangueraontour
To: pers-gx4zs-1600598017@craigslist.org
Subject: Dance Partner

Are you still looking? I might be interested.

From: ntinshoj
To: tangueraontour
Subject: Re: Dance Partner

Hello,

Thanks for responding. Yes, I am still looking for practice partners. I have a couple now, but I want to practice more. I am an intermediate tango dancer and want to push myself to the next level, which requires practice, practice, practice. I am from New York City, living here now. I do internet-related work. My Castellano is poor, but I am making steady progress. Tell me about yourself. Are you new to tango or have you been dancing for a while?

From: tangueraontour
To: ntinshoj
Subject: Re: Dance Partner

Hi,

I started dancing tango over five years ago in Calgary (Canada) and consider myself in the grey *intermediate* classification. This is my second trip to Buenos Aires. I'm staying at least until the end of the year, then plan to travel around Latin America. While I'm here, I'm soaking up the culture. I write, take photos, dance, and brush up on my Spanish.

I've taken some tango classes. I've mostly stayed away from *practicas* and *milongas*—mostly for lack of a partner. I'd like to get into the scene in a bigger way so a regular practice partner would be good for me.

I'm almost 5'8"—then add heels. How tall are you?

Maraya

From: ntinshoj
To: Maraya
Subject: Re: Dance Partner

Hi,

So, you have been dancing tango for five years? That kind of makes you pretty advanced, no? I consider myself intermediate. Some days everything works great, and other days I feel like a drunk kangaroo. I'm focusing on basics. However, I recently instituted a new practice policy with my teachers where they teach a form—a series of 50 or so steps that I learn over and over, much like the way martial arts practice works, and I work on my basics within that form. Right now I am working on opening with my right shoulder, which, for some reason, I find difficult.

My schedule is fairly open. I can make my own hours for the most part. I find most *practicas* I go to have turned into informal *milongas*, so, yes, if you are going to practice, it works well to bring a partner. It is for the same reason as you that I often don't go to *milongas*.

I am 5'7½ inches, and with my tango shoes, about 5'9". So, with heels, you may be a full two inches taller then me. I know this is a serious issue for some. If you like, we can meet first for coffee, talk for a while, and take it from there. What do you think?

I've attached a recent photo of myself.

Jesse

He looked respectable, dressed in a tux—which can make any man look good—shaved head and glasses. Short. Good thing since he definitely did not look like my type and I wouldn't have to worry about weakening and turning the dance-partner situation into a messy situation—difficult to extricate from.

From: Maraya
To: Jesse
Subject: Re: Dance Partner

Hi Jesse,

I wouldn't consider myself an advanced dancer at all. One of my favourite Tai Chi instructors used to call himself a beginner after 25 years of practice. I think it's the same with tango—a practice. As long as you're a beginner you're always open to learning.

I started over five years ago but the tango community is quite small in Calgary and I didn't dance regularly. I also ended up with partners who were beginners and I wasn't challenged. So, don't let that intimidate you. Often I feel like I don't know a damn thing when I get on the dance floor. My principle job is to follow well and that's what I need to focus on no matter whom I dance with.

I too have attached a recent photo—taken with my friends at Niño Bien. I'm second from the left. If what we want to know is whether we are going to be compatible dance partners then what we should do is dance—not go for coffee.

Maraya

From: Jesse
To: Maraya
Subject: Re: Dance Partner

Hi Maraya,

You're second from the left? Looks like I got lucky! :)

Your perspective is both refreshing and healthy. My teacher is trying to get me to absorb the whole 'Gestalt' of tango. It's as much a social protocol as a dance. He tells me I should get more comfortable with asking strangers and dancing with a wider variety of women.

Any time in the next couple days is good, so you pick a venue and off we go!

hasta luego,

Jesse

From: Maraya
To: Jesse
Subject: Re: Dance Partner

How about El Beso 2-3 tomorrow?

Maraya

From: Jesse
To: Maraya
Subject: Re: Dance Partner

Okay, see you tomorrow. Looking forward to it.

/j

CHAPTER 10

Follow the Bouncing Freckle

El Beso was a few short blocks from my apartment. I entered through the bright red door and ascended the wide, sagging, wooden staircase to the second floor. The room fit into one corner of Corrientes and Riobamba, with heavily-draped windows on two sides, a bar snug up against the dance floor, a mirrored wall, and a large squarish post near the center of the dance floor. The post didn't pose a problem for small classes, but during a crowded *milonga,* it presented an annoying obstacle. In the daytime, the tables were stacked and pushed away from the floor, making it more spacious than it needed to be for a class— when there were only a couple of students like there were today.

Moments after I arrived, as I was putting on my shoes, I heard the front door close, footsteps on the stairs, and my new dance partner appeared from the top of his shiny head—down. *Good, definitely not my type. I should be safe just dancing with him.* I didn't want anything to get in the way of the dancing—none of that messy relationship stuff. I didn't want anything to disrupt my "men-o-pause." But, as he walked toward me, he had a swagger that was attractive in a cocky, New York, street-savvy sort of way.

"Hey," he said, offering his right cheek, as I did mine. We went through the perfunctory Buenos Aires greeting ritual of air kisses.

"Hi."

As we exchanged formalities, names we already knew, the young instructor, Oscar, sauntered over to tell us there was no *practica* today.

"Looks like we're going for coffee after all," I said. "So much for our test drive."

"Oh, that's okay, I could use a coffee, something to eat. We can get to know each other and dance another time." Jesse lit up a cigar as we left the building. "I just quit smoking cigarettes," he explained.

Even though I hated cigarettes, I didn't mind the smell of cigars so much.

"Where do you want to go?" he asked.

"I don't know, I just moved to this area, don't know it well yet. Let's just walk until we see a place we like."

I was aware of his height as he walked beside me—determined to not make it an issue in our potential partnership, even if I were to increase the difference by wearing heels. In Buenos Aires dance halls, there was a multitude of men, some excellent dancers, who hovered slightly over five feet. It was only dancing. If I closed my eyes it didn't matter.

We settled on a large café a couple blocks away at the corner of Callao and Corrientes. We chose a table beside the window overlooking the busy intersection. Jesse motioned to the waiter for menus. There was a brief awkward silence as we perused the choices and gave our order. Jesse didn't take long to break the discomfort with his easy manner and ability to speak openly and directly.

"So what's your story, why are you here?"

"Here in Buenos Aires? I ran away from home." I grinned and paused. "I'm on a sabbatical of sorts. It seemed like a good time to go: my daughters are grown up and my parents are healthy. What about you?"

"I pretty much ran away from home too. It's a long story, but basically I came here because they have good heart healthcare and no extradition treaty. I love tango and I followed a woman here."

"Oh...hmm...sounds like a lot of story behind that."

"Yup." He carried on after he had me hooked. "I had a heart attack a few years back. I was on my bicycle, luckily right in front of a hospital in New York, so they managed to save me. Not so sure that was a good thing. I couldn't work so I couldn't pay my child support and pretty soon my ex had me in front of an unsympathetic judge. I decided I had to get the hell out of there. Andrea, my girlfriend, was moving back here so I came with her."

Good. He has a girlfriend. I watched his mouth move as he talked; a carefully manicured goatee encircled it. It made up for the lack of hair on the head; it looked good. *But why would he want to attract attention to his tobacco-stained teeth?* I became mesmerized by the cute little freckle on his upper lip and watched it bob up and down as he spoke. His bespectacled eyes seemed wise and kind, with pain behind them. There was a lure of mystery about him—his story—intriguing and sad.

The waiter arrived with our food. I stirred sugar into my *café con leche* and took a bite of my *empanada.*

"How is it?" Jesse asked.

"Good. I love the coffee in B.A. They make it exactly the way I like it pretty much every restaurant I go to. What have you got there, what is that? It looks like a breaded beaver tail."

"Ha, ha," he managed with his mouth full. "It's a *milanesa.* Pretty common here. I believe the Italians introduced it to Argentina. My mom used to make it—better than this."

"So, you're Italian?"

"Half."

"Your parents are still both alive?"

"Yup. Living in Arizona. I skype with them once in a while."

60

"Nice. Hey, how come you need a dance partner—doesn't your girlfriend dance?"

"Nah..."

"Doesn't sound like a good situation," I said, noticing his hesitation.

"It's not. We're not getting along so well. She's kind of hysterical. She keeps saying she wants to have my baby, and that's not going to work for me. I've got enough kids already and I'm not so good at commitment."

"I hear ya. I've got a similar problem. How many kids do you have? You must miss them."

"Sure do. Three. Two boys and a girl. She's thirteen—and totally acts like it, if you know what I mean. The boys are older. I think Sean will be able to visit me here when he turns eighteen. I won't be returning to New York any time soon."

"How come?"

"I've got those nonpayment of child support charges against me. I called the courts and told them where I am and why. But, they don't care."

"And with no extradition treaty, I guess you can just stay here without worry, right?"

"More or less. For now. I don't know what I'll do when my passport expires. But, hey, enough about me. What about you? Why Buenos Aires? How long have you been here? How long are you staying?"

"Been here almost three months. I planned to take about two years off from my regular life." I paused and fiddled with my coffee cup while I contemplated my next answer. "Why Buenos Aires? Hmm...I guess tango has a lot to do with it but I also just love this city: the architecture, the European feel, the grittiness, the culture—I love anything Spanish."

"The Latin men..."

"Well, sure, in theory, but I'm not looking right now. I need a break from men."

"So, you come here to dance? Sounds like playing with fire."

We laughed at my predicament.

"How 'bout kids?" he asked. "You got kids?"

"Two girls. They're pretty much on their own. Their dad was supposed to look after them while I was away, but he died."

"Oh, shit, sorry to hear."

"No worries, we'd been divorced for a long time."

"Still, that's gotta suck."

"Well, yeah, actually, you have no idea.... But hey, this is getting deep and depressing for a first 'date' so why don't you tell me about tango. Where do you like to dance?"

"I have my favourite places. I like Villa Malcolm, Practica X, Maldita and Bendita, Tango Queer. They all seem to have a younger crowd, more relaxed. I'm not into the afternoon *milongas* where all the geriatrics go. Too traditional for me."

"I don't know where some of those are, but sounds like we might be on the same page. I prefer the less traditional vibe myself. I've been going to the school in Galerías Pacífico, taking women's technique and ballet classes. At least those ones I can do on my own. There's a studio next door to my apartment where I've been going for yoga. They have a young crowd there and they seem to be more open-minded. Maybe we can check out a class there?"

"Sure. What's it called?"

"Estudio DNI. I'll check their schedule and let you know."

"Sounds good." He motioned for the bill.

"There's also an instructor I like at the Escuela de Tango in Galerías Pacifico. I think his name is Gustavo—"

"Naveira?"

"No, not him. But a similar style—*nuevo*."

"Oh, that sounds like fun."

"I'll look into that too."

We both left a few pesos on the table and got up to leave.

"Well, it was really good to meet you," Jesse said.

62

"Same here. I'm looking forward to a test drive."

"Okay, well just message me and we'll get together for a class in the next few days, maybe a *practica* somewhere."

We hugged and parted at the corner. I headed back to my apartment, a little lighter in step than I had been for a while.

I like him. I just hope he can dance.

CHAPTER 11

Scheduling

The single biggest problem in communication is the illusion that it has taken place.

George Bernard Shaw

From: Jesse
To: Maraya
Subject: Scheduling

I am working on my calendar and I forgot the exact time we are going to Estudio DNI on Saturday (it is Saturday, right?). Can you please remind me?

/j

From: Maraya
To: Jesse
Subject: Re: Scheduling

Hi Jesse,

Practica is from 3:00 to 6:00 on Saturday. We didn't set a time. What's good for you?

Maraya

From: Jesse
To: Maraya
Subject: Re: Scheduling

Three sounds good. Also, we should visit some of those places and check out the music scene they have going on ... and I am interested in pursuing the switched roles (you lead, I follow) so I think the gay practices are best for that.

/j

From: Maraya
To: Jesse
Subject: Re: Scheduling

Whoa there ... it all sounds good but let's see if we can even dance together yet. I don't want to learn the lead for a few months—until after I learn to follow better.

Maraya

From: Jesse
To: Maraya
Subject: Re: Scheduling

Okay :)

Thursday, I stood outside the Rodriguez Peña auxiliary location for the Escuela Argentina de Tango and waited for Jesse. He didn't come. Since I didn't have a cell phone, I couldn't call to check on him. It was only our first dance date so, although I was ticked off, I gave him the benefit of the doubt. Nicola had told me that Dan stood her up on their first date; she told him to take a hike. He had to work extra hard to regain her trust and she gave him another chance. Then, she married him. He's been very supportive throughout her illness.

From: Maraya
To: Jesse
Subject: Stood Up

Hi Jesse,

Did you forget about me already? We were supposed to meet at Rodriguez Peña at 8:30 tonight for a class and *practica*. When you emailed to say you were doing your schedule and asked about Saturday, I should have reminded you but I thought I would give you the benefit of the doubt before I started caretaking you. And, unfortunately, I don't have a phone, otherwise I would have called you. Oh well, see you Saturday at three—right?

Maraya

From: Jesse
To: Maraya
Subject: Re: Stood Up

Oh no!! I feel terrible! I thought we had just scheduled for Saturday. I guess I got all confused with the change in dates when we were at El Beso on Monday. When I was editing my calendar, I left Thursday out completely. I have to make it up to you somehow … oh, I know —I have an extra phone I can give you. You'd just have to buy phone cards. It'd probably be a good idea for you to have a phone.

/j

From: Maraya
To: Jesse
Subject: Re: Stood Up

Thanks! It would be great to have a phone. It would make things so much easier.

M

From: Jesse
To: Maraya
Subject: Re: Stood Up

Okay, I'll get it to you Saturday at 3.

/j

From: Maraya
To: Jesse
Subject: Re: Stood Up

Do I need to remind you?

M

From: Jesse
To: Maraya
Subject: Re: Stood Up

Let's see if I can tie my own shoes this time—but thanks for thinking of me!

/j

From: Maraya
To: Jesse
Subject: Re: Stood Up

Wear the ones with Velcro.

I liked his easy-going manner and the fact that we could kid around with each other. It was a comfortable situation and he seemed fun. They were important qualities in a dance partner, since we'd be spending a lot of time together. I hoped.

Jesse and I met at Estudio DNI, next door to my apartment, for a class with Pablo and Dana on Saturday. Mistake. Those two had just returned from a European tour and were wildly popular with the tango tourists. The old salon-style room, in what used to be someone's home 100 years ago or more, was far too crowded for our level of ability and our first time dancing together. It was hard to see the teachers' demonstration and Jesse got frustrated right away. He didn't seem to be patient with himself. We weren't off to a good start.

"Hey, let's go practice in the other room across the hall," I suggested. "There are a few couples over there and more space."

"Okay, good idea."

We practiced what we thought was the sequence and started getting comfortable with each other. It seemed to be a pretty good fit. Keeping it light and having a sense of humour would get us far. But, it would be a long road of persistence and patience to get good as dance partners.

From: Maraya
To: Jesse
Subject: After practica

I thought we did pretty well for our first time. What do you think? You seem to have good musicality—so whatever level you're at— you can dance. Some guys have taken lessons for years and can't feel the music. Your lead is also good—well-communicated. Now, we just have to get you to stop leading with your left hand. Don't be afraid to give me feedback. We're both here to learn. We should have a talk about what we need help with—our weaknesses, what we want to accomplish, etc.

BTW, did you say you were taking private lessons?

Maraya

From: Jesse
To: Maraya
Subject: Re: After practica

Thank you. I have been obsessing about that on and off all day! I left yesterday feeling quite happy with our dancing (more yours than mine), and with a stronger motivation to improve. It takes a little while for dance partners to sync up, at least for me. Once the communication starts to flow, we will have many constructive conversations. I think we make a good couple on the floor and I'm getting inspired.

I take privates once every two weeks, or more if I can afford it, with that teacher you met in Calgary, Damien. I alternate with a *maestra* who is heavy on technique. I recently started these classes, so I should be getting better pretty fast. Why do you ask?

/j

From: Maraya
To: Jesse
Subject: Re: After practica

You told me about Damien. I forgot—sorry. Is it once a week? Just wondering if we might take some other classes too—if there's a teacher you're interested in. Gustavo isn't back until August and he's the only one at this point that I'm interested in, but I hear good things about teachers from time to time. Do you want more Salon style, Milonguero, Nuevo? Not sure what Damien teaches.

M

From: Jesse
To: Maraya
Subject: Re: After practica

Why don't you come to my next class? Unfortunately, it's not for two weeks. Maybe we can go next week though instead. I'll check with him. He should be cool with it—with you coming too.

/j

From: Maraya
To: Jesse
Subject: Re: After practica

Okay, sounds good. I'll wait to hear from you.

M

Ж

My visa expired and I hadn't left the country in the past ninety days. I was officially "illegal." Although Linda and I had talked about travelling to Iguazu Falls, when it came right down to committing, we realized it would be more effort and expense than either of us wanted to expend. For me, it would've been an extra effort to get a visa and travel to the Brazilian side—to see the falls—but mainly to get my passport stamped so I could re-enter Argentina anew for another ninety days. My other option was to scoot over to Uruguay on the Buquebus for a day or two, perhaps see Montevideo this time. I didn't feel inclined to do a trip on my own right now. Nor did I want to see the most beautiful falls in the world without a "beloved." I wanted it to be special. It would have to wait.

A third option was to go to the Imigración Office in Retiro and navigate my way through the various queues, try to get my message across, and pay my hundred pesos and, hopefully, by the end of the day, gain permission to stay ninety more days. That was unappealing, and, when I discovered it was Flag Day, impossible: government offices were closed.

I'd heard that several people lived in Argentina for years without exiting every ninety days and without consequence. When I leave the country I will be required to pay a fifty-dollar fine—a mere slap on the wrist. Less than the price of a trip. The idea of being "illegal" kind of lent an edginess to my adventure that I liked.

Overall, the heavy stodginess of depression seemed to have lifted and I didn't feel like crawling back into bed all the time. I was still experiencing some vertigo. *Still off balance.*

CHAPTER 12

Birds of a Feather

From: Jesse
To: Maraya
Subject: Better with wine

I noticed that you seemed happier with your dancing after a glass of wine. I swear, wine is the secret to enjoying the dance more (not necessarily doing it better!). And, according to my mom, wine is also the secret to writing. You might want to try it.

My relationships suffer from the same ailment as my tango—too much in my head! But, I've made definite progress—with my dancing—not so much my relationships.

Any time on Thursday works if you want to do a class with Damien.

/j

From: Maraya
To: Jesse
Subject: Re: Better with wine

One glass is fine. More, and I can't dance or write.

A typical guy is "too much in his head" and a girl may be too much in her heart. We each have to find the balance. I haven't figured that out yet, since I'm usually drowning somewhere in my head. Frankly, I don't trust either one—head or heart—as they've both been wrong. I think going with the gut is best—although I haven't always had much luck with that either. I'm beginning to think that going with the left foot is probably as valid a choice as any. :)

Maraya

Damien had pushed the furniture back in the small salon of his mother's apartment. It wasn't the ideal space for teaching a lesson, but a lot of young people in B.A., trying to make a profession out of dancing and teaching, seemed to struggle. He showed Jesse a complicated sequence which we then tried to repeat, with only moderate success. I wondered if Jesse would remember it and repeat it later.

As we changed our shoes afterward, Jesse said, "I have time for a quick drink but then I gotta get to Andrea's. She insisted on making me pizza for my birthday."

"And you do what a woman insists?" I teased.

"Pretty much." He looked away, blushing slightly.

"I'll keep that in mind."

We went to the bar across the street from Damien's apartment and took a seat by the window. Jesse continued the conversation as we ordered a glass of wine each. "Yeah...I think this is the last time I'll see her. I can't take her outbursts. She's crazy. I'm tired of crazy but I seem to keep attracting it."

"You must like something about it. Lucky for you, I'm not crazy."

He smiled. "I don't know why I keep getting myself into these situations. They seem great at first and then they just implode. I'm lousy at long-term relationships."

"Maybe you want to consider short-term relationships if that's what you're doing anyway. Admit it, name it and go into it expecting it to last only a short while."

"Huh? I never thought about it like that."

"Well, if you're dating women who are just passing through Buenos Aires, or you're not staying, it makes sense. If you're not here permanently and they're not here permanently then why would you think you could have a permanent relationship?"

"Valid point. You mean instead of thinking and hoping something is going to work out beyond a year, knowing it never does, and I like to play the field and not commit, I should just be honest with myself and the women and declare the situations to be impermanent, as they really are?"

"I know. It's what we do and yet it's an outrageous concept."

"Hmm...interesting. I'll have to think on that.

We finished our drinks and shared a cab to my place where he dropped me off and went on to Andrea's for the rest of the night.

Ж

I had a dream I was surrounded by birds: small, tropical, colourful. I noticed more and more of them. The one that stood out the most was crimson with a plume and long tail feathers. It was the size of a cardinal, with a black beak. In its beak was a much smaller version of itself—like a baby but not babyish—just smaller. Some of the other birds had small versions of themselves in their mouths too. I thought I'd get my camera and take photos but I would have to move carefully so as not to startle them. I edged toward my bag, removed my equipment, but there was something wrong with my camera and by the time I was ready to take a photo, they were all gone. Several online sources stated:

It is a favourable dream to see birds of beautiful plumage. A wealthy and happy partner is near if a woman has dreams of this nature.

CHAPTER 13

Blackout

We're all about the same height lying down.

Jesse and I attended our weekly 3:00 class with Angus and Lucia at Niño Bien. They were a couple just starting to teach together —he was Irish and she, a *porteña*. Their newborn daughter Michele was always with them. They weren't well known but we started attending their class initially because I'd wanted Jesse to meet Cherie and Ruben at the Los Consagrados *milonga* afterward. The first few times we took classes at Niño Bien, Jesse had a date after and couldn't stay long enough to meet my friends. This week, we were able to stay for a while.

Ruben checked out my "date." "*Tu novio?*" he asked.

"*No, mi compañero de bailar.*" I made it clear that Jesse was not my boyfriend but just my dance partner.

Jesse soon admitted he disliked the scene at Niño Bien and wasn't interested in enduring it even if it was home turf for my friends. But he enjoyed the classes. Although I enjoyed my friends, I couldn't disagree with him about the stuffy scene. On the other hand, I didn't enjoy the classes. Often, we ended up the only students and received a private class on a huge empty dance floor. I liked that, but I didn't like dancing with Angus as he was even shorter than Jesse and he smelled. If it weren't for so many eager regulars arriving before the *milonga*, sitting at their regular tables each week, facing the dance floor with only us to gaze upon in judgment, and if it weren't for the fact that we disliked the canned music, we would probably have stayed longer. But, we often went to Dante's, a restaurant on the next block, to eat. Then, we attended another class somewhere else.

If we had time between classes, we'd walk to Jesse's tiny studio apartment a few blocks away and he would help me with computer stuff. We planned to burn some CDs today. Jesse walked his bike beside me. It felt good to have him to hang out with. Having a friend and a routine made me feel more comfortable about my decision to be in Buenos Aires. I didn't like to go out by myself, especially on a Saturday night, and I didn't enjoy returning to my empty apartment.

As we neared Jesse's street, we noticed the power was out in the entire block. Late afternoon of a southern winter, it was already dusky; the *kiosko* was open and illuminated by candles: business as usual. Jesse purchased a cigar, soap, and chocolate for me.

"The power's gone out several times during the eight months I've lived here," Jesse complained. "It's pretty frustrating when the computer goes down."

We entered his building. With the elevator out of order, we had to walk up four flights of winding marble stairs in the dark. My little travel flashlight came in handy. Jesse carried his bike and I carried everything else. That kind of exertion was probably not good for a guy who, less than a year ago, had had a heart attack. But we had no choice.

Unconcerned about security, Jesse had left the balcony doors wide open and the apartment was frigid. After closing them, he straightened up the sheets since the bed was the only place to sit. I wrapped a blanket around me, sat down and huddled up against the wall. Since we couldn't download any music with the power out, we were at a loss for what to do. Jesse lit candles and poured some wine out of an already-open bottle.

"It's the first time I get to use these new wine glasses. They were my only birthday present. The wine is kind of old. I hope it's okay."

"Did you have it in the fridge?"

"No."

"Smells like acetone. I could use it to take my nail polish off."

"Oh, yuck, gross!" He spit it back into his glass and went to the bathroom to rinse out his mouth.

I put mine down. Jesse returned and sat on the bed empty-handed. He looked at me in the dim light. I started giggling like a silly schoolgirl. Embarrassed, I named it: "...nervous laughter."

"Why?"

"Well,...because it strikes me that there is only one thing to do in this kind of situation."

He smiled and leaned in to kiss me.

Ж

From: Jesse
To: Maraya
Subject: Aftermath

You were very cute (and I mean that in a good way) last night. Thinking about it made me smile a few times today :) Too bad the power came back on so soon. :(

/j

From: Maraya
To: Jesse
Subject: Re: Aftermath

What the hell happened anyway? A power failure? More like a surge. I was cute? How? Five-year-olds are cute. I'm all unstrung now—and that's cute? My inner slut has been unleashed. I came to B.A. to hide out, take a *men-o-pause*, get focused, and that lasted about three minutes. I have so little discipline. Now I'm not going to get a damn thing done.

So, I was trying to figure out what I like about you and I think it has to do with the fact that you never tried to impress me, that you're not afraid of me, that you're open and authentic—and despite all your "foibles," or maybe because of them, you're particularly charming. I'm a wreck.

M

From: Jesse
To: Maraya
Subject: Re: Aftermath

Jajaja! Men-o-pause, very clever! Come on, you WERE cute, being all nervous and giggling. You were irresistible.

So, let me understand. You come to a Latin American country that is famous for sensuous, handsome, virile, arrogant, swarthy men ... to take a break from men? That's like me going to Cancun at spring break to get a little peace and quiet!

From the beginning, like the first time we spoke, it was clear to me that I did not need any "game" with you. I felt quite comfy and relaxed with you from the get-go. I feel we already have an intimate relationship, but without the usual string of stuff that precedes and succeeds such intimacy. This is new for me, and refreshing. Like you, I'm somewhat on a relationship sabbatical. The fact that I get to hold you close to me, to move your body, your breasts against me, to feel you receptive to my embrace, to feel us move together ... well, this has had a lot to do with feeling comfortable and intimate with you.
First off, let me be clear about one thing. Sex between us would be awesome! Yes, I guess it could be a distraction. I'm already distracted. BUT, I am not either in a hurry, or hold it as the most

important thing between us, so do not feel like there is an elephant in the room now. To be honest, I think it is inevitable that someday you and I will find our sweet and sweaty bodies entangled together in a delicious carnal feast of pleasure, but there is no rush. If this ever happens, it does not take away anything from our friendship, right? Perhaps I've said too much now … but it's so easy because I feel comfortable saying anything to you.

xjx

From: Maraya
To: Jesse
Subject: Re: Aftermath

Hey,

I guess you've been very well behaved then from what you've told me. Thank you for maintaining those boundaries—I admire that. Just waiting for an invitation, eh? So, then you managed to orchestrate an entire block blackout? Very clever. And what happened to me? No idea. I was surprised by my nervousness and giggling. How embarrassing.

xMx

From: Jesse
To: Maraya
Subject: Re: Aftermath

Hey,

Yes, I have been very good. No, I won't withhold or not share stories about any of the crazy *chicas* I might encounter, and I look forward to hearing any of the escapades you may have. We are big boys and girls, so unless you and I decide to come to some kind mutual agreement, I assume you will be out there having fun and I will cheer you on. And I will continue my mid-life crisis by chasing young and psychotic *chicas*. If you and I find something special to share then ... hallelujah! Honestly, I would find it refreshing and healthy to share our "escapades of love" with you like a friend. But, seriously, if you think this will cause a problem, then I will absolutely not cross that line ... :(damn!

xjx

From: Maraya
To: Jesse
Subject: Re: Aftermath

Aw,... you're so cute in a colon and parentheses kind of way :)

xMx

I never wanted to become a tango cliché: "Single woman goes to Buenos Aires to heal her broken heart through tango and falls in love with her dance partner." I've read that story before. Another broken heart usually ensues. I did, however, hear some success stories—women who stayed in B.A. with their new love. Anything is possible.

I was naïve to believe I could spend my entire time away—away from men. My so-called men-o-pause.... I was naïve to believe I could dance tango on a regular basis with a man, share meals and plenty of deep conversation, without becoming intimate. He believed we could, not only feel free to be with others, but also continue to share openly with each other. Maybe he could, but it would be a stretch for me. Experience suggests it wasn't likely to happen.

I could fall in love with him like I could fall in love with this city—grit and all—and against all better judgment. It would do me in. His apartment was messy, unkempt and even somewhat dirty—by my neurotic, North American female standards; his eating habits were atrocious—by my arrogant, health conscious, upper middle class propriety. His history, his current situation, his messed up life—all appalling. There were a lot of things we didn't see eye to eye on. He was not the ideal man for me and I was not his typical choice of woman. It would never work in the long run. But…we also had a lot in common.

I would only be in B.A. a few more months. I liked him, I enjoyed his company, I could communicate with him, he made me laugh. He was my dance partner and my friend. He could be my lover too—why not?

CHAPTER 14

Learning to Surrender

Two exceptionally tall women accompanied me up the tiny elevator to the class at Niño Bien. They must've been several inches over six feet. When Angus danced with one of them, his face was in her sternum. I'd say breasts, but she was so slim there was nothing to nestle into. How does a man steer his partner around a crowded dance floor when he can't see over her?

Jesse and I struggled with a simple pattern. Did they change it each time or did we keep seeing it differently and consequently not remember it at all? We always seemed to be famished by 4:30 when the class ended, and Dante's had become our regular hangout. We enjoyed the neighbourhood atmosphere and it was never busy at that time of day. They prepared a tasty grilled fish and Roquefort *empanadas*.

Over the hour, we chatted and watched the hooker outside the window unsuccessfully attempt to snare whatever little traffic there was on the quiet street. Jesse agreed we could teach her a few things about self-promotion.

"She could do a couple simple things to improve her chances, don't you think?" he said.

"You mean like comb her hair?"

"Oh, I dunno, some guys think messy hair is sexy."

"It looks like she just got out of bed from her last customer. That's never sexy. How about that skirt?"

"Only works if one can imagine nothing underneath."

"I always thought it would be a good social service to teach street people to do what they do with more self-confidence—like actually *expect* to get the hand-out, the john, or whatever."

"Personal development for street people…hmm…that's quite a noble concept. You mean, teach them to improve their life on the streets instead of trying to get them off?"

"Yeah, why not? Self-confidence, positive thinking, that's half the battle to getting what you want. Even if you don't have any, even if you don't feel it. Fake it till you make it—you know?"

He smiled while he chewed. Eventually, she moved out of our line of vision and onto a different block. We finished our meal and strolled to Jesse's apartment, stopping at the *kiosko* for a bottle of wine. He started burning some photos onto a disc but we ended up in bed. It was getting too late to make it to another class. It's difficult to move a tango from horizontal back to vertical, so we stayed put.

A beautiful sun-shiny day tried to coax us up as it peeked around the brick wall that was the view from Jesse's only window. Since there was no food in the apartment, we walked the block to King Sao and climbed the stairs to the third floor balcony. Overlooking the corner of Indepedéncia and Entre Ríos, we soaked up the winter sun…and it felt like summer. I was blissed out.

"I come here a lot," Jesse said. "I've had to repeatedly explain to them how to cook eggs over easy the way I like them. I think they've finally got it."

He ordered three with toast. I wondered how his heart felt about that. I ordered one egg and a fruit plate. We sipped our coffee.

"I keep having these dreams..." Jesse said, cautiously, as if testing my reaction, "...more like out-of-body experiences—they're so real."

"Oh, yeah? What about?"

"They're pretty strange. Otherworldly, so to speak."

"Go on." I tried to be encouraging, to let him know he could tell me anything.

"Well, it starts out where I'm being chased by some kind of space ship, I'm in one too, but the other one is bigger."

"So, you're in space?"

"Yeah, and I feel like I've done something wrong but I don't know what it is. They're after me—some kind of galactic police force. I don't know where to hide but then I see a dot in the distance and shoot toward it at the speed of light. It's a planet and I hit it, landing myself right in front of a gravestone that has my name and birth date on it. It was like I died from a life in another dimension that I had to escape, then was 'reborn' into this one."

"Weird...."

"And I feel like I have a mission."

"You have a mission here?"

"Yeah, but I don't know what it is!"

"You have any idea why they might have been chasing you?"

"Not really...but I feel like I was some kind of a resistor, a rebel of some sort, and they wanted to get rid of me. And they still do."

I wasn't sure what to make of it. Anything was possible and I certainly had no idea what was true and what wasn't—especially for someone else. Even so, I joked, "You know, they have medication for that kind of thinking."

"Thanks. I'm not that crazy. Weird shit just keeps happening to me."

"Okay, well hopefully, if they catch up to you here, them or the *actual* police, they'll leave me out of it."

"Yeah, no, they're not after you by virtue of your association with me."

"Good to know."

Parting ways mid Sunday, after spending Saturday night and Sunday brunch together, was difficult for me. I headed back to my apartment intent on decompressing. A short time later, I got an email from Jesse.

From: Jesse
To: Maraya
Subject: Happy sounds

Geez ... I've never heard the neighbours going at it before—like every two minutes. But then, I've never had those kinds of sounds coming from my apartment either. I think we started something. Maybe we spread a little love around beyond the walls. Now...she's singing...must be happy. :)

xjx

From: Maraya
To: Jesse
Subject: Re: Happy sounds

Me too :)

xMx

In the past week, since we've gotten closer, the dancing has been terrible: repetition of old worn-out patterns, forgetting, no new steps incorporated, asking but not getting what I wanted. I was bored and irritated. I was disillusioned with "enlightened" communication and we reverted to juvenile jousting—"no it's not, yes it is, no, yes"—until one of us finally stopped trying to be right, gave up, or started laughing. Laughing is good.

I couldn't even dance with other men—I felt like a klutz. *Practicas* are supposed to be places to practice but Jesse just did the same ol' same ol' and I became a stubborn Taurus ox resisting the lead. I wanted to go somewhere new. I started thinking maybe I should learn to lead. That way I could go where I wanted to go on the floor, in the way I wanted to express the music, and take someone with me. I could be the one in control.

Saturday, I arrived at Niño Bien early and told Angus I didn't want us to learn anything new. Jesse and I wanted to go over what we had already learned because we didn't remember it. Other students arrived and Angus showed the day's pattern, ignoring my request. Jesse liked the new one so we spent the entire class practicing it. I tried to stay calm and responsive. We were on display as the regulars trickled in and sat at their usual tables. It felt like a re-run of a bad movie.

At least we headed to the *parilla* on the corner instead of Dantes, intent on trying different food. I wanted to try *locro*, a traditional Argentine stew, but they didn't have any. It was only made to order for the next couple days because of the holiday. *What holiday?* So, I ordered a *merluza*.

I was probably hypoglycemic, pissed off that I couldn't get the food I wanted, and I got bitchy. We argued. I said I was bored with the dance and I needed him to learn new steps and incorporate them into our dance. He fought back; he defended; he didn't like the way I was talking to him. I shut down. He wouldn't let me—he encouraged me to speak.

I said, "You interrupted me and then made me wrong."

"You're right, I'm sorry. But, I hate it when you generalize when it doesn't apply to me."

"I'm sorry too." After a moment of silence and between mouthfuls I said, "That's cool, I'm impressed."

"About what?"

"The fact you can call me on my stuff—and not just hide out. I've never been with a guy who stood up to me. We fight pretty good."

Sometimes we were childish and our disagreements were immediate and raw and emotional. Sometimes we'd get exasperated and give up. We'd laugh and move on. It was over as quick as it started. None of that "enlightened" new age bullshit where we "owned our stuff" and intellectualized, felt into our hearts, took responsibility and didn't lay blame. None of those mature ways of communicating that I took years to learn and do well—sometimes—and then do badly. Relating devolved into something quite primitive around him. And it seemed to work.

We went to Jesse's place to get some CDs. He put on Bajofondo and we started to dance. Finally, music that inspired me. We were actually dancing, not "practicing." In that cramped space we could play whatever music we liked, not worry about negotiating floor traffic, not worry about getting it right or not remembering, and not be concerned about looking foolish in front of onlookers. Our own private *milonga* was so much more fun and relaxed.

"Do you still want to go to another class tonight, maybe a *milonga* later?" he asked.

"No, I don't think so. I'm having fun right here. What do you want?"

"I want you to have fun. I've having fun too."

We decided to cuddle and watch a movie. I'd planned to go home early but we ended up in bed.

"Relax," he instructed.

"I'm trying!"

"No 'trying'—that's antithetical—just surrender."

I focused on my breath and his hands on my skin while he reminded me to relax.

"I think I'd like to tie you up and blindfold you. Be my sex slave. Just open up and receive me."

"Umm...okay,...I guess...." I hesitated—flustered, not quite sure I was up for that. But I trusted him.

He got up and returned with a scarf. "There you go...good girl," he said, adjusting it. "Now,...isn't this fun?"

He was teaching me how to surrender, how to follow. I wasn't sure I liked it.

CHAPTER 15

The Mother Load

I'd been in Buenos Aires for about six months and was feeling good about what I'd accomplished. I'd made friends, and one special friend was also my dance partner, so I was getting out to practice. I'd started the Buenos Aires English Writers group. I looked forward to Wednesday mornings when I would walk a few blocks up Corrientes to the café—where writers from all over the world gathered to share work and tribulations with each other in the quiet café at the back of Centro Cultural de la Cooperación. The Buenos Aires English Writers group had a few permanent members and many other writers just passing through. We even had native Spanish speakers, anxious to get feedback on their English. Members were working on fiction, memoirs, and blogs.

One morning, Hank, an American script writer, said, "I sure would like a photo exhibition."

"That sounds like a great idea, let's do it." I blurted without thinking. I'm sure Hank hadn't planned on actually going through with his idea, especially as a joint project, but I was going to make it happen for both of us. I had no idea how, but a part of me seemed to know it could be done. It would make my photographic expeditions at the cemetery worthwhile.

I had met Brenda at a Newcomers luncheon. She was a *porteña* but had an American partner. Brenda managed the gallery her family owned on Calle Defensa in San Telmo. I mentioned my idea to her and, by some force of magic, Hank and I were offered a small room on the second floor of the gallery during the Festival de la Luz, an International Photography Exhibition in August. I was blown away with how easily it all came together. I was making Hank's dream come true in addition to my own. To top it off, my daughters' visit would coincide with the exhibition and our reception. They would get to see the culmination of my efforts and resultant success. It was worth feeling good about for sure. I found a print shop a few blocks away and a framing shop across the street from the apartment; I got busy choosing and framing my best work. It had taken a while, but I was feeling good.

Ж

From: Maraya
To: Jesse
Subject: abstinence makes the heart grow fonder

Hi,

We'll have to behave ourselves for a couple weeks. My girls get here tomorrow. Won't be much dancing—or anything else for that matter. Sorry.

M

From: Jesse
To: Maraya
Subject: Re: abstinence makes the heart grow fonder

No worries. We can go back to being just friends for the
time being. :)

/j

I desperately wanted my daughters to have a good time during
their visit. They hadn't travelled much, so it should be an exciting
adventure for them and not too scary since Mom would be there
to guide them and show them a good time.

I'd instructed them on how to get a taxi at the airport and
tell the *taxista* how to get to the apartment. I waited for them
downstairs. It was Sunday so there wasn't a lot of traffic and they
made good time. It was an emotional reunion on the sidewalk. I
collected both babies up in my arms and we shared hugs and
tears. We hustled their suitcases upstairs and they both flopped
out on the bed. It'd been the longest flight they'd ever had.

It had been a year since the girls' dad had died. It was fitting
that we would share the anniversary with each other. Not a happy
time, but a good time to be together. Rather than feign happiness
about visiting their mother for two weeks in a foreign country,
and how exciting that *should* be, they were comfortable enough to
show their true feelings—life pretty much still sucked for them.

I had a general plan for an excursion each day—a fun and
interesting activity. The apartment was far too small to be cooped
up in together for too long. But I also wanted to allow them
space to just relax and be themselves, to do whatever they wanted
to do…which turned out to be mostly nothing. Except sleeping,
they liked sleeping. I'd hoped we'd all sleep together—family bed
style—but since the "queen" was just two singles pushed
together, there was no "middle" for Mom. I let them have the
bed and I slept on the floor on a Therm-a-Rest in a sleeping bag
in my couchless living room.

We headed to Konex one evening after wandering through the Abasto Shopping Mall where we'd shared a familiar-to-them McDonald's meal in the food court. There was a line-up around the block. *What? For La Bomba?* This foreign mom with young daughters in tow asked the gatekeeper what was going on and somehow got us special treatment. We walked straight in to the already overcrowded event. The band was making a video recording—hence the interest. I had loved bouncing to the rhythms of La Bomba with Jesse in the past but we could hardly move in there and it wasn't much fun for the girls. We returned to Konex later in the week to see a live performance of "Rent" in Spanish. We'd all seen the movie in English so knew the story and didn't have to rely on understanding the words.

I treated us all to a "spa" day of sorts. First we went for pedicures in Recoleta and then for massages and waxing just a few blocks up the street from there. It's not what I'd ever done with them back home, but treating them in Buenos Aires was affordable.

I'd gotten us tickets to a tango show at the theatre in Galerías Pacífico. As we headed there along Calle Florida, I took a photo of the girls with the Obelisco in the background. Then we headed up the very crowded pedestrian street toward the theatre in the Centro Cultural Borges in the mall. With daughters in tow and a pack on my back instead of my over-the-shoulder bag, I looked like a tourist. When we arrived at the theatre and were waiting for the show to start, I dug around in my pack for my camera so I could enjoy all the photos I'd taken of the girls since they'd arrived. There was no camera. I thought my head would explode and my heart beat its way out of my chest. I was so upset that I couldn't enjoy the performance. I was supposed to be the protective mama bear, but I felt vulnerable and violated. The girls fell asleep while I stared blindly at the stage.

Luckily, I had transferred my cemetery images onto another disc prior to the girls' arrival. But, irreplaceable moments of my life with my precious daughters had been stolen. It's never about the equipment. I used Amanda's camera to record the rest of their trip.

Starbucks had recently opened their first location, in the trendy *barrio* of Recoleta. Something familiar. I dropped the girls off there and walked to Carlotta's for a session. I spent most it crying out of frustration, regret, grief and guilt...all the feelings I'd suppressed in their presence gushed out.

"It's been a difficult time for you," Carlotta acknowledged.

"Yeah. For a lot of different reasons," I admitted, wiping my eyes.

"Didn't you say it's the anniversary of their father's death?"

"Yes."

"Then I'm sure they're feeling triggered too. They don't have to pretend with you. They can be their authentic miserable selves. It's a gift you're giving them. Don't worry about them not enjoying Buenos Aires. They're here for you."

"I guess. Doesn't feel like it. Still, I wish I could do something to help them have a better time."

"Don't be so hard on yourself. Maybe take them shopping. They're likely to pick up small treasures that will remind them of this time you're spending together."

What twenty-something girl wouldn't love to shop in a foreign country? We walked up and down Corrientes, the Once shopping area. They tried to get interested in it and eventually bought a few items they were satisfied with. It was good we were close to the apartment because Amanda and I started to feel crampy so we headed home; we'd started to bleed at the same time, so stayed in for the rest of the day.

The reception party for my photo exhibition with Hank coincided with another reception in the other gallery space and the Sunday San Telmo Street Fair. I sent the girls to check out the fair while I entertained my guests. I'd had my drawing and paintings in exhibitions before but I'd never considered myself a "professional" photographer. I was so thrilled that I got just a little too tipsy.

When the girls headed back to Canada, I tried not to feel like I'd failed them. I tried to focus on my achievements. I'd had a photography exhibition in a major foreign city, during a major photographic festival. It wasn't really as big a deal as it sounds… but it does sound fantastic so I'm sticking to it. Check. I'd made good on a promise I'd made to my daughters and, even though the timing could've been better for them to appreciate it…it was what it was. Check. I had a thriving writers group. Check. I had a dance partner, lover, friend. Check. Other than my mother-guilt, I was feeling pretty good. Things were definitely looking up.

CHAPTER 16

El Mundial

Jesse and I had talked about getting together Friday night after the girls left but I couldn't reach him during the day. I was both annoyed and worried. He'd been complaining about chest pains and shortness of breath. I realized something could happen to him and I would never know. Late in the day, he sent a short text message that he was still on a conference call and he would talk to me later.

I went to the gallery to wrap up my photos and take them back to my apartment. I decided to go to Gallery Nights downtown; Jesse dropped by my apartment at the last minute and we went together. Hungry, we chose a *tenedor libre* around the corner from gallery row. I was in the bathroom at the restaurant and thought how nice it was to not have to bring up the matter of our relationship. I didn't like being the initiator of difficult conversations in my relationships. The men were often less than receptive, or capable, of having conversations about delicate matters. I returned to the table and, coincidentally, Jesse brought up the subject at hand. *Great minds...*

"Hey, you know what you said before about short-term relationships?"

"Yeah...."

"Well, I was talking to a couple buddies about it. One was kind of on the same page as me—never really having thought about it, yet operating in the same manner—one relationship after another. The other guy thought it made good sense—like you said. Especially in my situation, living here indeterminately, with *chicas* passing through."

"So, did you come to any conclusions?"

"Well, we seem to get along pretty well, even though there's a lot we don't have in common, and you're obviously going to leave and I'm going to stay—"

"Yup."

"So, I guess we're having a short-term relationship."

"Seems that way."

"And since we know we're not going to 'break up,' maybe we'll end it on good terms and we can remain friends."

"I don't see why not."

"Well, that'd be great because it's not usually the case for me. Usually there's a lot of tension and bad blood."

"I know what you mean."

"And this is the healthiest relationship I've had in a long time—maybe ever. Others appeared 'normal' and healthy and underneath they sucked. We might look mismatched, but I think the connection between us is healthy. We seem to communicate pretty well and we have fun together."

"I was thinking the same. I'm glad you're able to bring this up and talk about it. I hope you'll also be able to tell me about whatever's not going well."

"So far everything is going pretty well. I'll let you know."

"I'm not so good at bringing up stuff that isn't going well," I admitted, "so, hopefully between us we can work things out."

"Okay, deal."

Ж

El Mundial de Tango is an annual festival in Buenos Aires each August. Competitors come from all over the world. Several events are free of charge, organized and sponsored by the government. Live bands, classes and lectures were taking place in the empty Harrods department store on Calle Florida. Jesse stood in line for several hours to get two free tickets to each of the final events: Salon Tango and Stage Tango.

Luna Park was packed and the seats were uncomfortable. The competitor's dresses were stunning and the performances were technically incredible. I didn't envy the judges' difficult decision of choosing winners. The performances all looked flawless to me.

Afterward, we ran into Maria Teresa, Jesse's Spanish teacher, and her French friend, Jean Luc. Jesse bummed a smoke. As we walked toward Sunderland, I said, "You know, I don't mind cigars so much, but cigarettes are gross."

Before I'd even finished my sentence, he'd flicked it out onto the street not even half-smoked.

"Thank you," I said, kissing his ashtray mouth as a show of appreciation for his sacrifice.

We arrived at the club and they granted us entry before realizing we didn't have a reservation. It was already quite crowded but they brought out another table and a couple chairs for us. Feeling peckish, we ordered a pizza. It was gross, but dancing was fun. We made it an early night, which allowed us to secure a taxi easily as others were still arriving. We headed back to my place, and since it had been a long day, Jesse was exhausted. I was too.

Ж

From: Jesse
To: Maraya
Subject: Practicing with others

Hey,

I think it's important we practice with others as it is so easy to get used to a partner and get into bad habits. I especially noticed this when I was at Practica X last week and was terrible on the floor because none of the women danced like you.

I was thinking about you pretty much all day yesterday. I wanted to connect, but I also wanted to not instantly respond to my every whim because I can be overbearing and wearisome if I do not check myself. We have this "space" between us that I think is very healthy. I wanted to put that first, but you're still in my thoughts, a lot (and I like that I'm in yours).

besitos baby,

/j

It was like I had written it myself. I felt ripped when we parted. I was so full of emotion that I had to have a nap each Sunday afternoon just to settle my anxiety. I had to catch myself —to not immediately send him an email. I wanted more.

Ж

I'd looked forward to seeing Jesse at Practica X again. I was sure he'd come back to my place later. I missed him. The class never started before 8:15 but I got there at 8:20 and they were already practicing the sequence. He wasn't there. I was lucky to get partnered with a teacher from New York and we started to practice. Jesse arrived about fifteen minutes later. I stuck my tongue out at him and resumed my good fortune. I wasn't mad anymore.

When the class ended, my partner just walked away and we hadn't put the two pieces of the sequence together. I wanted to practice. Jesse continued to practice with his partner. Someone else, who hadn't been in the class, asked me to dance. When the song finished, Jesse was still dancing, but soon joined me at the table. We danced for a while but he wouldn't practice the sequence with me.

"Not here. Later," he said. He went to talk to some of his friends, then danced with someone else from the class. I guess I was supposed to just sit there and wait for a man to ask me. After all, that's what we do. He knew people and I didn't. Someone from yoga asked me. Jesse was still dancing. Once we got together, we tried to practice some of the things we'd learned but he'd forgotten what Angus had taught the previous Saturday, even though he'd gone over it repeatedly in his mind. Finally, we figured out most of it. By then, I didn't care. Patience gone, I was pissed off. He was tired. We danced poorly.

He'd brought his bike and had to get up early the next morning to work so he wasn't coming over. I seethed. He noticed.

"What's wrong?" he asked.

"Do you really want to know?"

"I won't know for sure until you tell me."

I listed all the reasons.

"Hmph.... I thought you were pissed off about something else."

He walked me the few blocks to my apartment in silence. He hugged me. It didn't matter: If the dancing sucked, it all sucked.

I couldn't put my finger on what troubled me. Jesse hadn't done a damn thing wrong; he'd just done his own thing and I hadn't liked it. He'd said I didn't appear to be angry at the thing he thought I was angry about. But I didn't ask him what that was and he didn't offer to tell me. We obviously had different perspectives about what was going on. Mine was my problem, but I didn't know why I'd reacted the way I had. Was I afraid we were getting too close? Was I not getting enough attention?

From: Jesse
To: Maraya
Subject: Expectations

Good morning Sweety,

I didn't sleep well, last night's altercation stuck in my mind. Something about it just did not sit well with me. There was something other than just a standard off-note moment that pop up in the normal course of relationships. And I think it was because I was effectively powerless to change anything. What I mean is, the things you were upset about were things I could not reasonably do anything about.

I say "reasonably" because, were we to relive the evening, for you to not be upset, I would have had to not gotten lost on my bike, not forgotten my steps, not danced with others and then, changed my plans at the last minute. The first two are totally out of my control. I did not want to get lost and I was upset that I had. And, it frustrates me, even more than it frustrates you, that I can't remember the steps. The third thing I could have changed, but wouldn't, because that's simply unreasonable; we've agreed that we need to dance with others. The last item had more to do with miscommunication than anything else. I had no idea you were expecting me to stay over last night. You and I have control over our communication so we can take responsibility for that not happening again in the future.

So, I realize that your being upset was, as you said, your issue to deal with, but it is more than that. The fact (usually) is that, in a relationship when someone says, "It's my problem," they really don't mean it. They just say that to give some plausible deniability to their acting out of their emotional or psychological "stuff." I do this myself. Everyone does it, because we don't want to feel bad all alone.

If this kind of a dynamic continues, the relationship ends up becoming manipulative because the two people end up having to operate around each other's issues. And because this dynamic plays

100

into our own insecurities, doubts, fears, etc. It can grow roots fast and deep. And who wants that?

These are my thoughts.

Are you up for Villa Malcolm tonight? Or perhaps Independéncia 572? Have you ever been there? I'll bring my overnight bag. :)

abrazo,

xjx

From: Maraya
To: Jesse
Subject: Re: Expectations

Thank you for your thoughts. I appreciate your sharing with me. How the hell can you be so smart about relationships and yet so unsuccessful at them?

One can always be hopeful that the white knight on his blue bicycle will rush right in and fix everything and make it all better. I'm aware of that fantasy and when I said it was my problem and you didn't do anything wrong—I meant it. Doesn't mean I liked it. Doesn't mean you won't be affected by it. Doesn't mean I don't wish you would just wave your magic bike wrench and make it go away.

I don't know exactly what happened. I don't know what's going on. The best insight I can offer right now is: I put too many eggs in one basket, made you a priority, became excited, hopeful, started to have expectations and became too attached I left myself vulnerable to disappointment. Then I started to feel resentful about it. When the dancing doesn't go well, nothing goes well. That can be shifted. Last night it wasn't.

I just want you to know that I'm clear you did nothing "wrong" and when you realized I was upset, you did a lot of things "right."

101

MARAYA LOZA KOXAHN

I'll see you Saturday at 3:00.

M

From: Maraya
To: Jesse
Subject: After processing …

I've had some more time to process this. I think I'm afraid of falling in love with you knowing it's going to end in a few months. That feels incredibly painful. I need to push you away. I need to protect myself. I can't surrender to you because I don't feel safe. Maybe I'm just upset because the dancing isn't going well, maybe I'm upset because I didn't get my way. If you want me to keep these things to myself, because you can't influence them, then, next time, don't ask me what's going on. If I tell you how you affect me—it's your responsibility to not take it on.

xMx

102

CHAPTER 17

Donde Hay Amor, Hay Dolor

We decided not to rush off to another class after our regular class with Angus and Lucia; we went for a meal and returned to Jesse's. The energy had been high and chaotic for the most part—arguments and issues we were both dealing with, phone calls and interruptions. I just needed to sit a while, relax and talk.

Jesse was due to start a new job with Kaveh that would require him to show up in person and manage the office in Belgrano most days. We agreed to lighten it between us, spend more time dancing with other people and doing our own thing. I came to B.A. to focus on myself and do what I wanted to do. And I got caught up in a relationship. *Nothing changes.* I felt it was important for me to take the focus off him and our relationship, especially since it had a time limit. So, I continued with my yoga, my ballet and technique classes, and took tango classes by myself. I immersed myself in Spanish and, not wanting to lose what I'd gained from a month's worth of daily classes, I got myself a private tutor.

It was tough to get up early to get to my ballet class—and it must've been difficult for others too because I was the only one who showed up. Alejandro greeted me at the door like an old friend. He scolded me several times during the class for thinking it was too early—my excuse from not coming regularly. My body remembered the moves; it all came back pretty easily. Maybe I had made progress. Since my Spanish had improved, I was able to carry on a limited conversation with Alejandro. I discovered I loved the discipline of ballet, even though that was the very reason I'd quit when I was six. I knew it would help my posture and balance and my tango.

I stayed for Aurora's technique class, which was packed as usual. Women from all over the world lined up to learn proper footwork and *adornos* from the *maestra*. With repetition, and lower-heeled practice shoes, it was becoming easier for me.

I grabbed a couple *empanadas* on my way to my Spanish lesson. My tutor, Vero, was a musician and graduate of philosophy. I liked her independent bohemian energy. She lived a couple blocks from my apartment so I headed home for a rest before heading to another group tango class with Maya in the evening.

I rang the bell at Caseron Porteño and headed to the studio at the back of the yard. I occasionally attended Maya's classes because they were "familiar" and because I liked her. But they were often pretty awful experiences. She had a weird following.

There was one little hunchback with funny eyes who jerked me around the floor, seemingly exasperated by my not following him the way he thought I should. I got so angry that I finally said, "You're pushing me!" and he sort of let up after that.

Maya appeared to have issues with him but, when he did not receive her suggestions about his dancing, she graciously laughed it off. Finally, she just said, "*Suavecito.*"

"*Siempre suavecito,*" he defended.

Are you friggin' kidding me?! Did he actually believe he was leading gently?

It was a small class so we all got a lot of personal attention. Maya's instructions to me were useful and I tried to remember them while I danced. *Relax. You're holding back your pivot. Keep your*

104

hips level. Bend your knee as you come through, weightless. Walk like you're walking on the street: heel first. Transfer your weight until it's even, then to the other leg, brush, close. Disassociate. Spiral yourself. To simultaneously think and surrender to the lead doesn't come easily, but that's what practice is for. Hopefully, my body would eventually remember on its own and I could just relax and follow.

Since there were more women in the class than men, Maya asked me to lead for the last few minutes of the class—yet hadn't taught me how to do that. *The basic. I should know that. Of course I can lead the damn basic.* I stumbled through it but the women didn't seem to appreciate my attempt at being a man. However, I got my first taste for leading and I liked it.

Ж

From: Maraya
To: Jesse
Subject: World spinning

My world is spinning, I feel dizzy. It only takes one glass of wine for my boundaries to dissolve enough to feel a bit sad that you're out dancing with another partner. This relationship is moving so fast.

xMx

From: Jesse
To: Maraya
Subject: Re: World spinning

Yes, things have evolved. We are much closer now. Surprised me a little, actually. I am sure we will go thru many more metamorphoses in the next few months.

xjx

From: Maraya
To: Jesse
Subject: Re: World spinning

I miss you. Sex is great but I like just sleeping with you too.

xMx

From Jesse
To: Maraya
Subject: Re: World spinning

It is the same for me. I like lying next to you. Our sex (for me at least) is a great pleasure, but I find more deep pleasure in holding you.

xjx

From: Maraya
To: Jesse
Subject: Re: World spinning

Never feel like you can't be outrageously spontaneous and call me in the middle of the night or just drop by because you're on your way home from dancing with somebody else and you're feeling lonely.

xMx

From: Jesse
To: Maraya
Subject: Re: World spinning

I would have preferred to see you this evening. I just did not feel right cancelling my other weekly *milonga* commitment. I felt obliged. I will not think twice about being spontaneous or outrageous. I promise.

My general well-being is still a bit stressed. I find myself getting tired quickly these past few weeks. Even now, at this early hour, I am fatigued and not clear-headed. I think there may be some depression involved. I had gotten to a fairly hardened point about my life and cut off all outside contact as I hunkered down. But being in a relationship with you has opened some doors and I am brought back to a place I'd left behind, and that comes with some baggage (this is a compliment to you by the way).

xjx

From: Maraya
To: Jesse
Subject: Re: World spinning

Oh, honey, I'm sorry. I know. Same thing is happening to me. Each new beginning, each potential new ending, brings us a reminder of all the others. I feel my sadness deepened. I'm sorry your wounds are re-opened. Everything begs to be healed. Let me know how I can help.

xMx

From: Jesse
To: Maraya
Subject: Re: World spinning

Thank you, dear, those words alone are healing. We will help each other, this I am sure of.

xjx

CHAPTER 18
Those Middle of the Night Phone Calls

I had enjoyed a pleasant dinner with my new friend Phil from Salt Lake City. We'd connected a week earlier through an expat site—both of us looking for like-minded friends. He was looking for more than just a friend, and when I told him I wasn't, he didn't want to meet me. I challenged him on that—suggesting, as expats, we not narrow our choices, but instead open up to spending time with people, enjoying good food and conversation. Curious, he complied.

We had a relaxed rapport through dinner. He seemed like a nice guy: smart, a retired lawyer, well-travelled, spiritual. When I asked him to tell me about his children he said, "I have six children; one of them is dead."

Nine years earlier, Phil, his wife at the time, their daughter, and her boyfriend, had been out together for a quiet family dinner in celebration of the daughter's birthday. Mom and Dad hoped the two younger ones would join them at a movie after, but they preferred to go out with friends instead. In the middle of the night, Phil received a call from one of his sons telling him he'd just been informed that his sister had been in an accident. Returning home from a party, they had been hit head-on by a drunk driver travelling against traffic on the highway. The boyfriend, who had been driving, hadn't seen the approaching vehicle as they rounded a curve beside an 18-wheeler. Phil's daughter sustained a fatal head injury and died at the scene. In Phil's mind, his daughter will always be twenty.

Back in my apartment, I luxuriated in my sleepy state, trying to make sense of the phone ringing in the other room. Five rings weren't enough to fully raise me. The thought of getting out of bed in the chill didn't appeal to me. Round two of rings signalled insistence. *Maybe it's NOT a wrong number.* It was 2:30 a.m. I answered.

"Hello?"

"I'm sorry." It was Jesse.

"No, no, it's okay. What's up?"

"Can you come to the hospital with me? I'm scared."

"Sure, I'll be right there."

No need for questions. Given what had been going on in the past week, I should have half expected him to call. For a few days, maybe longer than he was letting on, he had been experiencing pain in the area of his heart. With his own stethoscope he was able to listen to the irregular rhythm of its beat. He had other symptoms, reminiscent of his heart attack: dizziness and numbness in his fingers and toes.

Jesse had been waiting for secure legal status and enough money to have some medical tests done. All the papers for his *Documento Nacional de Identidad* (DNI) had been filed and it was just a matter of time. His American passport would expire in three weeks. Soon he would be a man with no country, a fugitive from his land of birth, and not legal enough in his country of choice to qualify for health coverage. And, he was, unfortunately, the owner of a heart announcing its "best before" date.

Quickly and calmly, I dressed, descended the stairs, exited the building and hailed a taxi. It was only a five-minute ride; Jesse was pacing outside his apartment building when I arrived. He got into the cab and directed the driver to Argerich, a hospital nearby in La Boca, and handed me the file folder containing his medical records so he could hold his chest. The hospital he'd been transported to by ambulance several months prior, when he'd had a similar episode, had been a hellhole in Jesse's estimation. And, even though La Boca was considered by some to be the original hellhole of Buenos Aires, where one must never travel at night, the hospital itself was a welcome oasis.

Full moon and the emergency ward of the hospital in one of the seediest barrios in the city, one might imagine a worst-case scenario. It wasn't like that at all; the hospital was quiet. In fact, as we entered, there was no one to be seen. It wasn't exactly a waiting room, more like a large entryway with no chairs. A group of uniformed women stood around in a small room off the entryway and gave us a dull questioning gaze. A man entered behind us with concern on his face and a bit of English on his tongue. The moment the nurses understood Jesse's symptoms, we were ushered down a hallway. No questions were asked regarding health coverage or any other matters you might otherwise expect from a North American hospital.

I clutched Jesse's file to my chest with one hand and held his hand with the other. Although scared, he was in good spirits. Having been through this before, he sort of knew what to expect. An attendant outfitted Jesse with an oxygen mask and a pressure cuff and prepared him for blood-taking and an IV drip. He administered one nitroglycerine tab to be dissolved under Jesse's tongue. The pill had an immediate effect and he seemed to relax. Then, a couple attendants moved him to the "Shock Room." "Cardio" had been scratched off the door but I assumed it was the Emergency Cardiac care room and, hopefully, not a room where they did electroshock therapy. A handful of beds were occupied by patients in various stages of repose—some hooked up to monitors. A nurse shooed me out of the room. So, I sat on the cold floor, against the wall, just outside the door. There were no chairs in sight, no vending machines, no magazines, and no

110

other means of distraction or comfort for visitors. Not your typical hospital.

I heard a group of hospital personnel inside the room attempting to communicate in limited English, and Jesse in limited Spanish, until they tracked down a bilingual doctor who seemed happy to make good use of his English education.

Jesse asked if I could be in the room.

"No," the attendant said, "it's not allowed."

They figured it would take a while for the results of the blood tests. Jesse asked if he could tell me that and send me home. So, they finally let me in.

He was still hooked up to an ECG. "You should just go home," he insisted. "I have to wait for the results and I don't know how long that'll take."

"I want to stay with you. I wouldn't be able to sleep anyway. I'll just sit here until they tell me to leave."

So we sat quietly, occasionally making small talk, joking around and keeping it light. The doctor returned to say the blood tests would only take about twenty minutes more and I could stay.

Soon, he returned with favourable results and performed a follow-up ECG. All results were normal; everything was good. But, they weren't able to answer Jesse's question: "If it's all good, why have I been feeling so bad?"

The doctor insisted Jesse make an appointment with his cardiologist for the following day and told him that if he experienced the symptoms again he should return to the hospital immediately. Jesse felt embarrassed, like the previous time when it had all amounted to "nothing," but I was glad they had, not only given him permission to return but, insisted.

We were ushered out of the room to an exit with no mention of billing or payment and were instructed to be careful out there—not to walk through the neighbourhood. We caught a taxi, dropped Jesse off, then me, and I went back to sleep as the sun was rising.

When I checked my email later that morning, this was in my inbox:

From: Jesse
To: Maraya
Subject: DOOM!

Yeah baby! Feeeeeel the dooooom!!! Let it in! Surrender to DOOM! DOOMDY DOOM DOOM! All praise Shiva, lord of DOOM! Surf the DOOM! All aboard! Next stop...DOOMTOWN! As Jesus said, "Give unto Caesar what is Caesar's and give unto DOOM what is DOOM's" to DOOM or not to DOOM. That is the question. Whether 'tis nobler to suffer the slings and arrows of outrageous DOOM, or take arms against a sea of DOOM. Why did the chicken cross the road? DOOM!
O my Luve's like a red, red DOOM
That's newly sprung in DOOM
O my Luve's like the DOOM
That's sweetly play'd in DOOM!
~ Robert "DOOM" Burns
I saw the best minds of my generation destroyed by DOOM, starving, hysterical, naked.
~ DOOM Ginsberg.

Clearly the man was crazy. I liked that.

CHAPTER 19

The Fall of the Sparrow

There is special providence in the fall of a sparrow.

William Shakespeare, *Hamlet*

Jesse had had a rough night. He'd woken up in pain and it just got worse throughout the morning. So he took himself to Hospital de Clínicas in Recoleta for tests. The tests revealed that his veins were 90 percent obstructed; the doctors wanted to go in with a camera through his femoral artery to get a closer look and possibly insert stents. Jesse was re-prescribed anti-hypertensive and anti-cholesterol medication—neither of which would help solve the immediate problem—and nitroglycerine tablets for emergency relief.

Maria Teresa, the Spanish teacher whom Jesse had befriended, was at the hospital filling out forms when I got there. Jesse had called me to do it but I told him I wasn't confident enough with my Spanish to fill out important forms. The staff didn't appreciate his restlessness and inability to do nothing—as he'd been instructed. They told him he couldn't leave. They said he would remain under observation until the camera catheter procedure could be done and he would have to pay for it. He would eventually be moved upstairs once a bed became free.

Jesse told them he had to go home and take care of financial matters if he were to undergo any procedures. They said *I* should go home and get the money. We spent almost an hour trying to get them to understand how it was going to work.

Finally, Jesse understood that it wasn't that he *couldn't* leave, just that they wouldn't take any responsibility for anything that might happen to him if he left their care at this point. He would have to sign a release. He was welcome to return Monday and should be prepared to stay, and pay, or go to another hospital where services may be free but less immediate.

Ж

The pain came and went but Jesse wasn't going to let his condition stop him from having a good time. It was Thursday and we'd planned to go to Villa Malcolm. I didn't like the place much, so had to talk myself into going. I hadn't taken a class all day and I needed to move my body. I got off my ass and went for a massage and a coffee, hoping that would get me through the evening. Then I went to Jesse's to make dinner.

"I'm so tired," he complained.

"We don't have to go dancing," I said. "I don't care too much about it one way or another. It's been a lazy, good-for-nothing day."

"I do want to talk to you about how I've been feeling but I just can't right now."

"No worries."

Frustrated with our low energy, and after much deliberation, we went for a walk and got ice cream. Then we returned to his apartment and attempted to dance; we practiced exchanging the lead. Bad idea. We just got upset with each other. Neither of us had enough energy to move out of our respective comfort zones of lead and follow. Arguing is not real seductive and not usually good foreplay. But, we went to bed and the negativity evaporated.

Later, while we were lying in the silence before sleep, I whispered, "I don't want to lead you."

Jesse said, "Yeah, I've been thinking about that too."

Quiet for a few minutes, thinking his response didn't make much sense, I realized he thought I'd said, "I don't want to *leave* you." I felt no need to correct the miscommunication.

That night I had a dream: A little sparrow came into the room Jesse and I were in. Initially it seemed out of its element but then it gave Jesse one little peck with its beak in the middle of his lower lip. I thought that was sweet and said, "Oh! It kissed you!" Then it came to me and started to gently chew on my left brow. I thought that was weird. I carefully took the little bird in the palm of my hand and felt its softness; it didn't resist. I thought I needed to find it some water to drink. *Do I feed it with a dropper? Do I let it drink from a puddle outside?* I headed to the kitchen with it. The scenario ended and I woke up. Curious about the meaning of my dream I searched the web. I discovered that the sparrow has long been regarded as a bird of love, spiritual connection and, often, one of the most lustful and sexually active birds. Or, according to Shakespeare, it's a symbol of impending death.

Ж

Jesse experienced pain and pressure in his chest any time he exerted himself—cycling, dancing, sex. Headaches were a regular thing, as was fatigue. It had been going on for about three months, about the length of time we'd been together. I joked that it was my fault.

When he'd had an orgasm the previous night, he'd felt a sharp pain in his heart area. I saw that as an opening to discuss what I'd never discussed with anyone before. A bit tentatively I asked, "What am I supposed to do if you die?" This was not a conversation I wanted to have but I supposed I should know since I was spending a fair bit of time with him.

"Well, you're the closest I have to a significant other here," Jesse said. "You can contact my friend Ruth in the States. She'll know what to do about contacting my family."

"What about your body? How does that work with your situation here? They can't extradite you if you're alive, the U.S. only wants you in order to put you in jail. So, how does it work if you're dead?"

"I don't know, but it doesn't matter. My body can stay here, get cremated, put in a pauper's grave, whatever they do with people like me. I don't know, don't care. Don't worry, you won't be responsible for figuring it out."

Who would? "What about your kids? They should have some place they can go to grieve you."

"Nah, they don't need that. Don't worry about it."

I knew they did. My kids had taught me that when their dad died. But I could tell he didn't want to talk about it anymore so I dropped it. Hopefully, he'd be okay.

CHAPTER 20

Hot, Sweet and Spicy

I had based my wardrobe on the past three rainy days and now found myself uncomfortably warm in the sunshine. My toes were unhappy prisoners in cotton-wool-blend socks and sensible boots, and the rest of me was also hot and sweaty, as I walked the fifteen blocks to Jesse's from Boedo where I'd had lunch with Cherie.

There's something delicious about dropping in on your boyfriend on a warm afternoon in a foreign country. Jesse's work in Buenos Aires often continued beyond the end of the workday in New York; I caught him in the middle of a conference call. I settled down on the bed with a book—a little distracted by thoughts of my limbs around him, pulling him to me as soon as possible. My naughty thoughts continued to spread the flush I felt from my walk.

I had spent a lovely two hours with Cherie, catching up on the latest tango gossip. We discussed our writing. She'd been transcribing her unpublished memoir into a script for television. We talked about the steadily-rising prices in the city.

"I don't really like this city," she complained. "The prices just keep going up."

"So why do you stay? Especially since the change of seasons wreaks havoc on your allergies."

"I can't afford to live in Los Angeles anymore," she said. "Besides, I love Ruben and I love tango. I'm here because of love."

We talked more about love—hers and mine.

"For two years," she said, "Ruben and I fought like hellcats. I used to throw his stuff out over my balcony. But, I'd wanted to dance with him the first time I saw him. I waited every week for about a year before he finally looked at me. He's old-fashioned; I could never have asked him to dance. He took me out onto the balcony at Niño Bien that first night we danced, and he kissed me. I love him but he drives me crazy sometimes. And he snores. Are you in love with Jesse?"

"I don't know. He's not exactly my type—whatever that means. But, I've been in love with guys before who weren't my type. I'm not sure I know what love means anymore. I thought I knew but I've been in love so many times and it has always ended badly...or at least ended. I don't have much faith I could get it right with this guy. I don't want to be stuck in Buenos Aires because of love. I think I need to leave soon. It's only going to get more difficult to be with him if I stay."

"I know what you mean...." she concluded with a faraway look in her eyes.

The end of the Jesse's workday came soon enough. He'd forgotten about my visit and had taken the relief of a stressful day into his own hands, so was unable to fully participate in our lovemaking. I wasn't about to complain; he was attentive and generous. Sex was interesting with him and had become more so as we'd grown closer.

The neighbourhood seemed to get quiet as I got louder. But I was paying others no mind; I was wrapped up in the rapture of our community of two. I shed tears afterward—a release of all the pent-up bittersweet feelings.

We needed to eat before the *milonga*. I remembered Kashmir, one of only two Indian restaurants in Buenos Aires, was close to Villa Malcolm, and suggested we have dinner there. In this bland land of ham and cheese on white, my taste buds screamed for spices. We hopped a bus and hoped we'd recognize the restaurant along the way since I wasn't sure exactly where it was. We overshot but doubled back on foot.

I was tantalized by the aroma and the authentic decor. We were seated and Jesse had barely opened the menu before he slammed it shut. "Mutton Vindaloo," he declared.

"Give me a chance to enjoy the menu."

"No hurry, take your time."

"How will you know what you might want to order another time if you don't look any further on the menu?"

"Mutton Vindaloo every time. Do you think they make it spicy?"

"Spicy enough. I don't like it so hot that I can't taste all the subtle flavours."

"I do. I have a high tolerance for spicy."

"You're in the wrong country."

I took my time, and salivated over every item on the menu. I knew I wanted lamb—I just didn't know how I wanted it prepared. I asked the waiter, in hesitant Spanish, why there was no *chai* on the menu. I didn't understand his explanation so just nodded politely and proceeded to complain that the other Indian restaurant in town also did not have *chai*, yet, I knew the spices were available in a tea shop on Corrientes.

Unable to waste any more time imagining each menu option, I settled on Lamb Biryani. Our *servicio de la mesa* arrived to further whet our appetites: small rounds of naan with four kinds of condiments. *Perfecto.* The start to our culinary adventure looked promising; I was confident the meal would not disappoint.

Meanwhile, we drank whatever beer was on tap and chatted while we waited.

Without the expected delay of carefully prepared Indian food, the copper bowls of Lamb Vindaloo and Lamb Biryani soon arrived. The waiter surprised me by saying the cook was brewing *chai* for me and it would be ready by the end of the meal. I was so happy that I wanted to jump up and hug him.

"Mine's not spicy enough," Jesse immediately complained after his first bite.

As if on cue, the waiter brought a tiny dish. "More spices," he said. Extra curry paste did the trick.

My Biryani was superb; tender lamb and spices, a perfect blend of flavour and heat. From my first forkful I celebrated with a quiet mantra of appreciation. From the center of my tongue, to the middle of my torso, and out to my limbs, the entire afternoon settled upon me in an exquisite glow of pleasure.

"I think I'm going to have another orgasm," I whispered.

Mouth full, Jesse smiled.

Throughout the entire savoury portion of my meal I anticipated the sweet, spicy, milky, soothing, warm *chai* being thoughtfully prepared for me in the kitchen. As I forced myself to the point of discomfort to finish every morsel of my substantial meal, the waiter came by to say my *chai* was ready and would I like it now?

"*¡Por supuesto!*" I was more than ready for the finishing touch on a perfect day. I sipped and savoured slowly, grinning like a Cheshire cat. Jesse had another beer and we sat in contented silence.

We left the Kashmir and walked toward Villa Malcolm, several blocks away. Jesse smoked a cigar while I held my stuffed, complaining tummy. We caught a cab for the last few blocks.

The *milonga* was not crowded. At least we would be able to make our way around the dance floor.

"Why do you like this place?" I asked.

120

"I don't know. Why *don't* you like it?"

"I don't know. Bad energy or something."

The music was dull and our dancing—uninspired. Maybe there had already been enough perfection for one day. Jesse was tired and I was bored so we decided to leave shortly after arriving.

"You staying over?" I asked as we strolled down the sidewalk. Jesse nodded. "Oh, nice, I didn't know. What time do you have to get back in the morning?"

"The cleaning lady is coming at ten."

"Perfect. I'm seeing an afternoon movie with the ladies. We're meeting at noon."

We grabbed a taxi to my apartment and were soon curled up together in bed. Falling asleep always seemed easy for him. Not so for me. But, after a slow descent from cloud nine, I finally managed to drift off.

Even before Jesse got up to go to the bathroom in the night, I found myself awake and alert in the dark. Mind in first gear, I lay in bed, convinced I would fall back to sleep shortly. But, after realizing I would disturb him each time I moved, I got up and spent some time at the computer.

Meanwhile, he slept easily on my half of the bed. We would sleep in the middle but two single beds pushed together only simulate a double bed and that doesn't work well for two "consenting" adults. So, because we like to sleep entwined, I left him to sleep on my side alone. Soon he'd be up again to use the bathroom.

As I sat alone at my computer in the chill of the living room in the middle of the night, I reflected on the dissonance in my heart. I contemplated leaving this complicated city and my complicated relationship before I, too, became a prisoner of love.

CHAPTER 21

Magnification

Love does not obey.

Krishnamurti

My six months in Ray's apartment on Corrientes came to an end and I had to move as someone else was moving in. Linda offered her extra bedroom. Although it had suited my mood, I'd been in the *media luz* of the older part of Buenos Aires too long. Twelve floors up on the corner of Scalabrini Ortiz and Santa Fe allowed for lots of light to enter my room. With my magnifying mirror, I was reintroduced to each pore on my face. *Ugh!* An unwelcome sight. Eight months of Buenos Aires' dust had blown up from the streets and permanently lodged itself in my complexion. I saw a reason to have less light in my room. I closed the blinds.

Jesse seemed uncomfortable around me these days. He felt vulnerable. His heart hurt, and he was worried he would be rendered incapable of dancing and making love and just general daily activities. He didn't want me to witness that, or to help him. He only wanted me to see him at his best—or at least—his better than worst.

"You are completely loveable," I told him. It was easier than saying "I love you." Offering love in his "unworthy" state wouldn't ease his anxiety; it would probably increase it.

He began to cry, unsure of exactly why. He didn't want me with him. But, truth be told, yes he did. He had been so strong, so alone and scared for so long, that he wouldn't even admit to himself that he wanted someone with him. "This is the second time you've made me cry," he accused. "I've been waiting, watching, expecting, and, maybe even hoping, for a red flag to appear," he continued, "for a reason to look forward to ending this relationship on the grounds that there was no way it was going to work. There's been nothing."

"What would a red flag be? What would it look like?" I asked.

"There's lots—lots of excuses for it not working. The ones I know, the ones I'm used to, the ones I expect—like, if you were to shut down and not discuss what was important to discuss. Or, if you were to start blaming me for your experience. That's a couple."

"You haven't seen those," I said, "because I worked hard to heal those kinds of behaviours and I think I pretty much have them under control. There was a time when I shut down for years, blamed others. I know how ineffective that can be. Besides, just wait, it's early and I'm still on my best behaviour." I smiled sheepishly.

"I'm embarrassed. I'm probably at the lowest I've ever been in my life—except for right after my heart attack. I hope you get a chance to see me in better form before you leave."

"I'll be back," I said, though I wasn't sure why I was trying to sound reassuring. We didn't need red flags to know our relationship was temporary and would never amount to anything.

I got out of bed, unable to sleep again. I was disturbed by my own thoughts: *When do you say I love you?* It wells up inside me so many time—while making love especially—and I have to remind myself that love and sex are not the same. It wells up inside me when I look at him—vulnerable and strong—and I have to remind myself that love is not caretaking, but taking care of. It wells up inside me when I think of leaving him—never to see him again—and I have to remind myself that love is not desperation and loneliness. It wells up inside me when we have a stimulating conversation, and I am engaged by his radical thinking. I've found a kindred spirit. It wells up inside me so many times and I push it back. It is too strong. I'm frightened. And I don't want to frighten him. I don't want to appear to be making a commitment—one I'm not likely to keep.

I returned to bed and he snuggled up to spoon me and nuzzle the back of my neck.

"Sorry, did I wake you? I couldn't sleep," I whispered.

"No, that's okay. What's wrong?"

Hmm...I'm afraid...to tell you I love you."

"Tell me," he said, pulling me closer.

"I love you."

"I know. I love you too."

It had to be gotten out of the way.

The next morning, as we got ready to go out, Jesse pulled something out of his pocket and held out his hand. "I want to give you these," he said as he placed a set of keys in my palm. "Just in case something happens."

It wasn't an invitation or a commitment; it was a safety measure. Locking oneself out of one's apartment was a real possibility. Travellers were often alone in foreign countries with few friends, no trustworthy neighbours, and no place outside to hide an extra key. And Jesse, given his medical condition, might not make it to a phone or a door on his own should he need assistance. There was a possibility that, one day I might go over to his place, find his lifeless body, and have to deal with it. So, to receive a boyfriend's keys was more a responsibility than a gift. That's how we look out for each other. That, I think, is what love is.

124

CHAPTER 22

Independéncia

We decided to check out Independéndia 572, a *milonga* named after its address—at least that's what we called it. We had to duck under the steel door to enter the ancient building situated next to an auto-mechanic shop. The old house was rumoured to have been owned by Che Guevera's grandmother at some point. Not sure if that was true. It didn't matter. It was a good story. The house had a raw, mysterious air about it I found fascinating.

It was quiet when we arrived at the top of the wide, sagging wooden staircase. No one was around so we peeked in on the class, already underway. We were ushered back to the entrance by an old, compact gentleman with wavy white hair escaping his beret. He had a woollen scarf wrapped tightly around his neck and a bulky button-down sweater. I realized we'd have to start dancing if we wanted to stay warm in there.

We paid the "poet" our *entrada* and headed to the big room at the back of the house. There was a monstrous drawing of a reclining nude woman on the wall beside the entryway. The colour of the poorly painted walls gave the impression that heat was being emitted. Old photographs and drawings were scattered about the vertical surfaces. The bar was situated at the back and an old piano graced the dark, dangerously worn wooden floor.

Other than the small class, the room was empty. We chose a table for two on the far side of the dance floor and ordered a bottle of wine.

The class ended and the group sat together, more intent on visiting than practicing. We weren't about to waste an opportunity to have the floor to ourselves so we got up and started dancing.

"It's Saturday night in Buenos Aires and we're in some obscure *milonga* on the edge of San Telmo, the only couple on the floor. It doesn't seem real."

"I know, nobody would believe it. I wonder what's wrong. The weather's good, the music is good, where is everybody?"

"Kind of blows the stereotype, doesn't it?"

"You mean—the one where you can't move on the floor because it's so crowded?"

"Yeah, that one."

We sat down and nursed our wine. "Well," he said, "I suppose they could do a little work on the place to make it more appealing. Like, get an electrician in here."

"What else would you do?"

"If it were my place?"

"Yeah, let's say it was your place. What would you do to improve it?"

"I'd get some live music, maybe a singer, a piano player. I'd feature some dancers, hold parties, I'd definitely add some *nuevo* music to the playlist, and some non-tango music—maybe some blues."

"That's what I want to do! I'd love to go back to Calgary and just have a totally alternative *milonga*. That's the music that makes me feel like dancing. Any kind of music that's danceable. I'd like to be able to dance tango to any kind of music."

"I like that we have that in common." He grinned.

After an hour, two more couples arrived. We had to circumvent them on the floor but, other than that, we felt license

126

to dance our own way—which seemed more free and expressive than usual. Jesse had gained more confidence with his lead. The night was strange and fun—our own party on someone else's dance floor. More space than at home. It was surreal, like a movie set, as if we'd created a *milonga* in Buenos Aires and nobody came. I felt a little wacky, maybe because I was tipsy. I had trouble behaving as a proper follower and kept breaking free to express myself. I wiggled around and did pirouettes across the floor.

"Are you on drugs?" Jesse asked.

"No baby, I don't need to get stoned to have a good time."

"Well, unfortunately, I do," he said as he popped a couple nitro tabs. He was determined to keep dancing through the pain.

"Listen, we don't have to stay, I'm okay if we leave," I assured him.

"But I want to stay. I like it here. I'm having a good time." He was angry that his body wouldn't obey his desires.

After another *tanda*, he flopped down in his chair with a pained expression on his face.

"Let's go," I insisted.

CHAPTER 23

Outside Interference

I had originally planned to stay south for the winter but it was only my girls' second Christmas without their father. The holiday season, even though it had lost all other appeal for me, still seemed like the time one *should* be with family. So, a sense of obligation, guilt, and homesickness propelled me to make plans to go north. Jesse was still waiting to find out when his exploratory surgery would be; I didn't want to leave until I knew he would be taken care of.

Maria Teresa phoned Jesse to say she was in the neighbourhood and just happened to run into a charismatic healer, a Catholic priest, and could they come over and sit with Jesse for a while?

"Sure," he said to my surprise. I think he just had trouble turning her down since she'd been so helpful with translating for him.

The "healer" turned out to be just an ordinary traditional priest bent on saving Jesse's soul Catholic-priest style. Maria Teresa and I sat politely on the bed in the tiny room to witness the ensuing "miracle."

"Allow Jesus into your heart. He died for your sins." A little splash of water and anointment with oil. "You are now born again and all are blessed." *Yadda, yadda, yadda.*

"They meant well," Jesse said after they left. "It can't hurt."

"Okay, so now that you've been made new, born again and redeemed and all that, maybe you won't need surgery. Did you ask him if it'd be okay if we have sex?"

"He said we'd have to get married first."

"Did you tell him you're still married to someone else?"

"No, we didn't get that far in the conversation."

Out with the archaic traditional and in with the new and occult all in the same day, we expected the tarot card reader and her translator to arrive within the hour. Jesse was more inclined to use the wisdom of this type of "healer," as was I. It would be the second time he'd seen her; he obviously thought there was some value to her insight. I'd had some experiences with tarot card readers myself, and, therefore, remained skeptical. But I took the opportunity to have my cards read—since she was coming to us anyway and I could use all the insight possible.

The reader didn't speak any English and her translator wasn't much better. I went first while Jesse went outside for a smoke. From what I could surmise, I was told I would be called to return home in a hurry but I would be back to Buenos Aires. *I already knew that.* I was warned not to take the trip to Mexico I was planning; someone at home would need me. I was frustrated that there wasn't any more useful information from the translator about the reading.

I left the room while Jesse had his reading. Once the women left, we had a brief exchange about what had taken place.

"She said I was going to meet my soulmate," Jesse said without making eye contact.

Going to? So, I guess that's not me then...of course not...why do I keep trying to make this into something it will never be? "Oh." I couldn't think of what else to say in that moment. I felt conflicted. *What exactly is a soulmate anyway?*

Jesse got on the computer and made some calls to New York. I started to feel ignored.

"Any more girlfriends you need to call?" I snarled, after what I deemed to be too long. "I know they're your friends, and they're not here, and you need to talk to them, but I *am* here and I'm having a hard time with this too, you know. I just need to be a bitch for a bit."

He didn't give my mood any attention. After a few minutes I calmed down and went to him. "I'm sorry." We held each other. "I don't want to go home tonight, I'm too upset, I'll just fume at home. I need to shift this. Besides, it's easier to leave you in the morning than in the dark of night."

"Stay."

So, I did but I was distant, disconnected. I wanted a strong physical connection yet was afraid. He wasn't. He reached for me playfully and I tensed up.

"I didn't shower today," I said as a way to put him off.

"I don't care, I like the way you smell. I want to lick you. Tell me you want me to lick you."

"No, you can't. I'm a dirty girl."

"Tell me."

"Oh, no, no, no, you can't. I'm a dirty, dirty girl."

"I like the way you taste," he countered, voice muffled.

"I did some research," I said pushing him out of the way so I could straddle him. "It's a good idea for a man with a heart condition to be on the bottom."

"Yeah...that doesn't really work for me."

"Do what you must then, but don't you go and die on top of me, Buster!"

He rolled me off and onto my back and mounted me. He paused a couple times to slow his heart rate and allow me to catch up. He had opted out of pre-empting an angina attack by taking a nitro tab because they gave him a headache. So, as he concluded, the expression on his face was that of both agony and ecstasy. It hurt to make love. Comparatively, I felt way better, less bitchy. It was just what I'd needed.

"Whatever happens," he said, "you have turned out to be one of the most significant people in my life."

"I feel like I'm just passing through. I got into this situation on a particular premise and it quickly got out of control. Now I'm here for a specific purpose, to help you through this medical problem, and then I'm gone. We'll both move on brokenhearted, heal and meet others."

"You make it sound like we'll never see each other again, never talk."

"That's probably for the best. We always knew this would only be short term. It doesn't make sense to keep hanging on."

"Well, I'd hate to see you go out of my life for good. Don't try to figure it all out now, you don't know what the future holds. Let's just enjoy each other while we still have time together." He wrapped his arms around me.

Soulmates come in and out of our life for different reasons, all for our evolution. Some stay for a few minutes, some for days, others for years, and then they're gone, maybe to return in another lifetime. They don't always come in the package we'd like them to; the lessons learned aren't always pleasant. In fact, lessons that bring discomfort often offer the opportunity for the most growth. And, isn't that why we're here? Isn't that why we're together? To offer expansion and help each other through the process—to make the journey through life just a little easier for each other?

CHAPTER 24

Encroaching Flood

We picked up Jesse's reports from Hospital de Clínicas in Recoleta and took them to Hospital Argerich in La Boca. After being in and out of hospitals and back and forth to the lawyer's office and home and back again to the hospital to prove that Jesse was a resident, they booked his surgery for two weeks hence. They told him to bring his own stents if he wanted them to be put in at the same time as the exploratory surgery. Recent budget cuts meant they did not carry a supply of stents in the hospital. Two weeks would be a long time to do nothing but wait. It had been too long already.

Now that Jesse's surgery was scheduled, I could book my flight home. The days were getting longer and the weather warmer. The jacaranda trees that lined the avenues in the better neighbourhoods were in full purple bloom and smelled heavenly. It was easier to feel optimistic with the sun shining. But, when the temperature got to thirty degrees for several months, as it soon would, I'd be glad to go through hot flashes in Canada's cooler climate for a time.

After our Saturday class, Jesse and I headed to King Sao for a bite to eat. It started to rain. I didn't mind getting a little wet because the heat had been stifling. By the time we walked two blocks, I was ready for a warm *café con leche*.

When we arrived, the kitchen boy was pulling the tables in from the sidewalk and putting away the awnings. He had made no progress with trying to clear the sewer on the corner to encourage the water to take its natural course rather than enter the restaurant. Stubbornly, the water kept rising, up over the sidewalk and through the front door. We chose a table on the main floor so we could watch the encroaching flood.

After we'd ordered and were waiting for our food I said, "I want to tell you about the dream I had last night."

"Sure. Go ahead."

"I dreamed I'd returned home. I had a new man with me, but I could only *sense* his presence beside me. We were cleaning trash up in the yard. I said let's go across the street to the church on the corner. There was garbage strewn and the grass was tall and sparse like a wild area and there were broken CDs and garbage. I thought it was odd and unbecoming for a church. For a moment I was inside somewhere and the man, previously only a spectre at my side, was now smack dab in front of me and crystal clear."

"Anyone you know?"

"No, I didn't recognize him. But he's definitely someone I'd *like* to know. Anyway, I looked at him with great amazement, appreciation, like how could I be so lucky? I felt deep love for him. Then, I was back outside by myself."

"He disappeared?"

"Hang on, I'm not done. There was a new car parked on the lawn of the church. I wanted to leave, to drive away, but I wasn't in the driver's seat. There were ambulances, other emergency vehicles, and cars surrounding the area. I was blocked in; it ticked me off. I got out of the back seat to find out what was happening. Several people were hanging around—drunk and acting inconsiderate. A man in another car told me to watch out —they were all around my car—leaning on it. It was a four-door and three doors were open. I was beside the driver's side now

133

and it appeared I was going to drive. People were sitting in the back, legs sprawled out, just relaxing, and I told them all to get out. I was quite indignant that all those people thought it was okay to use my car. The drunk woman in the driver's seat said, 'NO!' and I grabbed her, yelling, 'Get the fuck out of my car!' I pulled her out and hurled her onto the middle of the street where she lay face down. I got in behind the wheel. By this time, some vehicles had moved and there was room for me to drive away. It was dark and there were no lights on the drive shift indicator. I thought I knew where 'D' was but I moved in real close to try to see it better. I managed to get the shift into drive and I left."

"Wow, you sure got aggressive. What do you think that was about?"

"I don't know. Let me finish. There had been an 'injury' to my car on the right side—damage like a bullet hole. I got on my phone right away to get quotes and make arrangements to get it fixed. It could be repaired, buffed and painted for $180."

"Whoa. So weird. That's how much it's going to cost me to get my stents."

"I know, eh? So, I'm driving down a narrow passageway by this time. I pass the woman, unconscious in the middle of the street. Another car stopped, maybe they thought she was dead, but I didn't care to help her; I hated her and was disgusted by her."

"Did she remind you of anyone?"

"No. Then I remembered I had to go back and get my boyfriend from inside the church. I drove backward down the narrow street and just barely missed scraping the car on the cement wall. I backed up a short distance and my guy came out from some doorway and got into the passenger side of the car and we left. That's it."

"Well, that's funny you dream that exact amount. I wonder if the 'injured' car was supposed to represent me."

"What? And I'm driving you?"

"I dunno…maybe I'm the 'vehicle' you take to get to your next boyfriend."

"Cute. Yeah, that's likely it."

Our food arrived and the floor was now flooded. The torrent showed no sign of abating and the kitchen boy had given up trying to direct the water. I sat cross-legged with my feet up on my chair. We were safe for the moment, and even enjoying the spectacle, but eventually we'd have to attempt an escape. Even if we'd wanted to take a taxi the two blocks to Jesse's apartment, the few floating by were already occupied.

"How will we get back to your place? It doesn't look like it's going to clear up any time soon and we can't stay here all evening," I said.

"We'll have to make a run for it."

"More likely a slog. There's at least a foot of water out there and there's no way I'm getting my Birkenstocks wet," I stated indignantly.

"Well, there's no way you're going out there barefoot. There's all kinds of broken glass, nails and other crap on the sidewalk. It's not safe."

"I guess you can't piggy-back me, eh?" I was stubborn—which led us to argue for a while. Exasperated, he offered his socks and we struck a compromise. We paid the bill and splashed home in the rain; he complained while I turned it into an adventure.

Ж

A week before I was to fly home, I had to move from my luminous twelfth-floor bedroom in Recoleta to the core of a *manzana* in San Telmo since Linda's daughters were coming to visit her for Christmas. The family-operated *hogar* was accessed by a long corridor from the street; its only natural source of light was a small interior patio with high walls reaching to a patch of sky.

The window of my tiny room looked out to another room, which looked out onto the patio. There wasn't enough light for me. I could lose perspective. I wouldn't know what time of day it was, or what the weather was doing. I couldn't live like that for more than a week.

The guest room on the other side of the paper-thin wall, was inhabited by a *tanguero* from Germany. He intended to take Gustavo Naveira's week-long workshop as did I. It takes a talented dancer to transcribe one of Gustavo's sequences. Wilf was a more advanced dancer than me and I was thrilled he'd agreed to be my partner for the week. I would otherwise not have been able to attend the classes. We would be able to practice in the small salon in our *hogar*. I would return to Canada fresh from having accomplished one of the many small things I'd wanted to do while in Buenos Aires—a class with one of the fathers of tango *nuevo*.

I had tried twice before to attend one of Naveira's classes. But I didn't know anyone skilled enough to accompany me so I'd arrived alone. Although the gender ratio was balanced, I didn't fare well with what was left in the way of a leader. In order to get any benefit from the class, a leader had to be an advanced dancer and a quick learner. Naveira demonstrated an intricate sequence repeatedly and couples were left to their own devices to remember and repeat. There were so many of us that the *maestro* was not able to provide much individual attention as he circulated. Lucky for me, Wilf was an excellent dancer and by the end of the evening we had mastered the entire sequence. The next night, we did it all over again with a new sequence.

So what? Maybe Wilf would be able to take some of what he'd learned and incorporate it into his dance but when would I ever dance that sequence again? Never!

After class, Wilf headed to a *milonga* and I entered the deserted streets of San Telmo alone. No taxis ventured to this end of the *barrio* at night unbidden and I had no numbers in my phone since I was used to hailing, not calling. I started walking and kept looking for a taxi to happen by, but eventually gave up. It wasn't far from one end of San Telmo to the other.

I was either stupid or fearless. No one would condone a single woman on foot through San Telmo at midnight. I wasn't naïve, nor was I afraid. With an elevated mood, I walked boldly down the empty street. If I could've whistled, I would have. Trouble could just as easily find me in the middle of the day, in any *barrio*, if trouble was what I was attracting; I wasn't. I found the dark and the silence rather comforting. It seemed surreal, as if it were my own deserted movie set. It was *my* movie and no one was going to violate my space and ruin my script.

Yes, it's possible I was an idiot—but I did make it back safely without even a suspicious glance. After all, even though we are bombarded with bad news, it comprises only a small portion of the overall news—which is mostly non-news. My news was, after an intoxicating tango class, there was nothing further to report.

CHAPTER 25

Rattling Keys

He shows up in my subconscious whenever he pleases,
and enters without knocking.
He still has the keys to that house.

Alice Steinbach, *Without Reservations*

From: Amy
To: Maraya
Subject: Home for Christmas

Dear Mommy,

I'm so happy you're coming home—you have no idea. I've been
having a really hard time lately. I don't know if it's just cuz it's this
time of year or what, but it feels like everything is going wrong and I
just need you to be here.

Last night I put in my two weeks notice at work cuz I couldn't deal
with the bullshit any longer. I think it'll be better now cuz I have
motivation to go out and get another job now cuz I HAVE to. I also
broke up with Jaden last night during work cuz we've just been
fighting way too much lately. So that was hard but he called me like
a 100 times last night and got a little out of hand with some stuff
but I finally told him I might be willing to try and work things
out...once again. I don't know if I made the right choice but if things
go back to how they were then that's it.

I've also been having a lot of problems with Dad not being here. I was talking to my friend Steph today, she took me out to a bunch of dealerships to look for a car. We were just talking about spirituality and stuff and she goes to see this lady who reads spirits or something and I want to go see her. I've lately been kinda feeling like Dad's presence is still here. I'm not looking forward to Christmas and my birthday coming up. Anyways, I don't wanna worry you but I'm glad you're coming home. Only four more days! I love you Mommy. See you soon. Have a safe trip!

xoxo

From: Maraya
To: Amy
Subject: Re: Home for Christmas

Hi Sweetheart,

Last night was the full moon; it makes people crazy. I'm glad you gave your notice AND that you broke up with Jaden. Don't let him wear you down. Tell him you need some time to think—that you're going through a hard time right now and you need some space. AND TAKE THAT SPACE! Not only does every place you will ever work have bullshit to deal with but so will every guy. Jaden will not likely change. He'll behave for a while and then it will be back to the same thing. You don't need that.

Dad is definitely watching you. There are a lot of spiritual readers around and some are better than others. You can start by asking Dad to come and visit you in your dreams at night. He did that with me for a while, unasked, even before he died. It was like we were healing our relationship at night on a spiritual level. Then, one night, after the four of us had a family movie night in my dream, he said he wasn't coming back—and the dreams stopped for a long time. Just last month he came back. He'd lost weight and looked good and said he felt really good. He said he'd had a trauma (yeah—he died!) and that going through it had created positive changes in his life. He had a nice house with an amazing view. Cathy seemed to be there in the background. I thought—Wow! Nice house, nice guy—and I was considering getting back together with him. Dreams are strange but if you're open to them they can give you lots of insight and healing.

I'm not worried, honey, you're doing great. You're moving forward. I was worried before when you were kinda stuck. Now I'm excited. Everything will be fine—really. I don't like Christmas either. We can hate it together.

Love you lots! See you Tuesday,

Mom

CHAPTER 26

Embracing the Darkness

I am out with lanterns, looking for myself.

Emily Dickinson

After a long, uneventful flight, I landed safely in a winter wonderland. The beautiful purity of freshly fallen snow was like a clean slate after the humid, gritty inner city with its pollution—visual, audio and olfactory—and frenetic pace. I felt like I could breathe normally again. It was so quiet that empty airwaves echoed deep inside my ear canals. But, the stark contrast also reminded me of what I'd left, and that I had not yet significantly changed my future.

Christmas travellers who'd departed after me were stranded, strewn about in airports with strangers, as the snow continued to fall relentlessly; we were embedded in a week-long deep freeze. I hibernated in my parents' basement bedroom since I had leased out my own home for two years. Home—crisp, safe and pristine —was probably the best place on the planet for me to have hot flashes. But, it got dark by late afternoon and I found that depressing.

My period came two weeks early, red on white, its arrival marked mine. It didn't take long before I spontaneously burst into tears. I missed Buenos Aires. I missed Jesse. I was so messed up. I didn't know where I wanted to be, nor where I *should* be. I had intended to travel to Mexico, then spend the summer in Calgary and return to Buenos Aires in the fall for another year or so. But that was so far away and too long to wait. Even though I was with my family, I didn't feel like I belonged here—not right now. I didn't feel like I belonged in Buenos Aires either. I didn't know where I belonged.

I'd needed Jesse to show me what was important: the practice of love, the easing of the journey of another, being in service. Not running away from difficulty, but facing it, immersing oneself and embracing it. I needed him to remind me I'm not the same person I was and that I didn't have to keep getting lost in my past.

From: Maraya
To: Jesse
Subject: The Unbearable Darkness of Being

Hi Hun,

I had a good flight—all went well. I felt disconnected upon entry and now feel like the whole thing was a dream. Except for the colour of the walls, everything is the same here. It feels so familiar and so foreign. What am I doing here? What do I do now? I cry spontaneously. I still grieve but it's for something different now.

This morning, dark, blowy and snowy, I awoke in (Argen)time to hear the DJ play "The Tango I Saved For You"—one I had never heard before.

I think you're right. I think I will miss you more than I thought. When I think about how much you've meant to me in the past few months, I can't believe I came home. Yet, I feel it was the right decision. I'm content to be here for now. You've helped me cement what I believe to be most important and now I feel adrift. I'm scared I will easily fall back into my old life. I need you to keep being my forceps. I need help to keep moving forward so I do constructive things with my life, and I think your encouragement and support have been such a gift.

I need some down time and then I'll talk to you in a few days—okay? I hope you're well.

love,

xMx

Ж

It's Sunday morning and I miss sitting outside an outdoor cafe enjoying the sunshine, intelligent conversation and brunch with my lover. My life at home is so different—almost completely opposite at the opposite end of the globe. This somehow satisfies my moon-in-Gemini spirit. I am content to be here for now and see what it brings me.

It's too cold to go dancing—and there probably won't be many dancers there tonight anyway—so I may wait until after the holidays to re-emerge. There is much to do—moving pictures and words around my computer and on pages and (hopefully) out to the world. There are many people to catch up with. My brother and wife arrive tomorrow and the others on Christmas Day.

Ж

From: Jesse
To: Maraya
Subject: Re: The Unbearable Darkness of Being

Darling,

Your sweet words are uplifting in this time of darkness—dark because all my technology is dying, leaving me crippled. My computer fried AGAIN today, this time for good.

I am glad to hear that you are content there. That's as good as it gets, no? And I miss you, dear, and the things we did together, even when we did nothing together.

I am going to Practica X tomorrow ... alone ... where I will bite my fingernails and nervously look for someone to dance with.

Going to bed now. I'm so tired and a bit anxious. The twitching has returned to the right side of my face. I need to relax.

Besos,

/j

Ж

From: Maraya
To: Jesse
Subject: We should break up

Hi,

I feel alone. Lost. Lonely. I don't feel connected to you. I write to you and you don't write back. You don't appear to want to engage to any great degree in a written fashion. You seem to prefer Skype. I don't like Skype. I acknowledge and appreciate that you *want* to call every day. Thank you for the effort. I get upset when I miss your call and don't know whether to call back or wait another day. I don't want to hang around my computer waiting for you to call. I don't want to be keeping tabs on what time you come home—or whether you come home at all.

We knew this would be strange and difficult. It's not working well for me. I need my lover. I don't know what we are, what we want to be. And because I'm not clear on these things—I don't know how to relate to you.

I can't see how it can do anything but get harder, worse and more confusing. Maybe we should cut our losses. You may want to rethink why you're such a bulldog when it comes to letting go of people. We can say goodbye ... and maybe we can say hello again. In the future.

Maraya

From: Jesse
To: Maraya
Subject: Re: We should break up

Dear,

I don't like thinking in terms of "together" or "broken up" or the baggage that comes with those concepts. Everything is always changing, you can create a new conscious decision in each moment. I have worked quite hard to get to this place of understanding because, in my darkest hours, I saw that this was the only way out, the only way to live with as little pain and suffering as possible. So far, I am happy with this view of the world, even though at times I long for stability and other comforts for the ego.

You know I prefer not to write emails, and tend to keep them short and to the point when I do. It's not personal. I'm not ignoring you. The emails I write to you far exceed those I write to anyone else in length and number. But I do hear you, so I will put the effort into writing you, in a thoughtful way and we'll also skype—as it's my preferred mode of communication. It's as face-to-face as it gets right now.

/j

From: Maraya
To: Jesse
Subject: Re: We should break up

Hey,

I suppose it's not true that if we "broke up" we'd never talk again, but maybe not for a while. If we keep talking to each other like we're still "connected," it just makes it harder. I thought breaking up, shedding some emotion and attachment, then coming back unfettered would make for an easier transition—so we could get on with our "real lives." But you want to keep hanging on in this old way and I am so sucked into you right now that I can't even imagine being with someone else or having a normal life and if you go out with another woman I'm going to want to fucking kill you. At least if you were an ex-boyfriend it wouldn't bother me. But you ruined the chance of that happening by being so "New Age" about it. Quit being so enlightened.

Besides, breaking up doesn't have to mean forever. It's like a time out until such time that maybe it becomes a time in again. And while I'm thinking about it, and I'm tearing a strip off you—so to speak—anyway, I gotta tell you, new girlfriends hate it when you hang on to old girlfriends—especially the ones you say broke your heart. If they are friends, then talk to them like friends and not like lovers. If you are with a new woman and you start talking to me the way you talk to Enoka when I'm with you, you're going to have a problem—and she may not be as understanding as me—or whatever it was that stopped me from hitting you in that moment.

Okay, well, sorry about that. Looks like I needed to vent. Thanks for being tolerant.

Maraya

From: Jesse
To: Maraya
Subject: Re: We should break up

Hey,

You know, I am not trying to be "enlightened." I am trying to make life simple, but it seems to have the reverse effect.

146

From what I can see, of what you have said, "breaking up" doesn't mean anything other than a shift in your thinking or perception— right? If we "broke up," we'd still talk? I could still confide in you? We'd do projects together? If the answer to all the above is *yes*, then, for fuck's sake, let's break up! If only to make your life easier. For me, nothing will change. For me, saying we are *this* or *that* just complicates things because no matter what we say or do or promise or expect, we are going to be whatever we are going to be. And if either of us wanted to "do" something else, we would want to do that regardless of what we called ourselves. And, if we didn't "do" those things simply because of those labels, then we'd be lying to ourselves.

Look, you have been with other lovers in the past, as have I. Did it affect the way you and I were with each other? You and I may never see each other again, or find ourselves together living happily ever after. I don't know what will happen and I refuse to speculate because this is just what makes me crazy. And let's say we did end up "together." There is no guarantee it will last forever. Every day the relationship is either nurtured or starved, and even if nurtured, may grow into something you choose to walk away from at some point.

I told you I'm not prepared to enter into a "permanent" long-term relationship, to "settle-down" emotionally. I didn't say that because I wanted to play the field and have sex with whomever crosses my path, nor does it imply that I do not have deep feelings for you. I miss you, a lot. I said that because my entire concept of a relationship, up until recently, has been dysfunctional and fucked up, and I don't want to fall into that old world again. So I make no promises to anyone—and I have to fight the urge to. There is a part of me that WANTS to make you promises, that WANTS to say we are "together," and it creates some anxiety in me to force myself not to, but the part of me that wants to say that is the part I am trying to exorcise from my life. Most people would find this unacceptable— to be with a person who cannot promise them anything. I understand that.

I realize I will always have a problem with new relationships because I WILL talk to you like you are someone I love and I won't pretend it's not the case in front of my new GF (hypothetically speaking). If the new GF doesn't like the way I talk to you, then she has to decide how she will deal with that, and not expect me to accommodate her by forcing me to speak to you in secret. But, as I am resolved to the possibility of living single for the rest of my life, I do not feel the need to change myself to smooth her ruffled feathers.

I don't hang on to old GFs. There are a number of exes who will back me up on this. But, there are people in my life, like you, whom I share something more important than the fact we had sex. You and I had relationship long before we started conjugating and the reason we started was because we DID have a relationship. So, now that we are no longer conjugating, we are left with what we had in the first place, which is worth keeping. The women I "hang on to" are people I want in my life—like Ruth and Agnes. I hang on to them quite strongly even though we were never lovers. The fact is, I do not WANT to let go because they are part of my life, and they do not want to let go of me because I am part of theirs.

Wow. I was really chatty tonight! Sweet dreams, sweet woman.

xjx

From: Maraya
To: Jesse
Subject: Re: We should break up

Yes, you were quite chatty. Felt like a bit of a rant, a bit defensive ... but thanks.

xMx

From: Jesse
To: Maraya
Subject: Re: We should break up

148

Hi,

I was not feeling ranty or defensive when I wrote. In fact, I was feeling good about how I was expressing my thoughts and feelings, and it just all came out. Sorry if you don't like how I am trying to manage my life. Maybe I am scared. I don't even know myself.

You know what I want? I want my fucking life back. I don't want to be an international vagabond, I don't my bank accounts and credit card frozen, I don't want the law after me, I don't want to be illegal in Argentina, I don't want to go to jail, I don't want to have to work for an asshole because I have no choice. I want to see my kids, I want to build the most basic foundation of a life, I want to regain my footing, I don't want to be sick, I don't want to wake up every morning questioning everything I have ever done, I want to know I am not going to be homeless next month, I don't want my children to live in a house with no heat or electricity. I am not playing with your heart. YOU are. You are putting it through the ringer. Don't blame me for that.

/j

Ж

From: Jesse
To: Maraya
Subject: Radio Silence

Hello?

I haven't heard from you for a while. I guess you're still pissed off at me. I'm not sure why. I didn't say anything I haven't said before. I put my thoughts together more coherently, I thought ... as much for myself as for you. So, what does this mean? Are we no longer communicating? You tend to shut down and shut up when you're upset, but I do not want to second guess what is going on with you. Can you tell me?

If you don't respond, or respond with a one-line reply, I'll assume, for now at least, you'd rather not communicate with me at all.

CHAPTER 27

It's Just A Cough ...

Nicola was breaking in her second prosthetic leg. The first one hadn't fit well. She sat on the bench in the foyer of my parents' home and removed her limb. Although it fit better than the first one, she wasn't yet comfortable with it. One day, you're skipping school and getting stoned together and—in the blink of an eye—you're both middle-aged and your friend is removing her leg because of cancer. I felt like I'd been away far too long.

We settled down in the living room with some tea. "How are you feeling?" I asked.

"Not great. It's been frustrating trying to get used to a leg that works."

"I bet." I felt awkward. I didn't know how to talk about cancer and amputated limbs. "Your hair looks great by the way."

"Thanks. You never know what you're going to get after chemo."

"But other than that, are you feeling okay?"

"More or less. I think all the complementary treatments are helping my body get back to a new normal." She took a sip of her tea. "How's it going with Jesse?"

"We're fighting. I thought we'd just end it and be done with it when I left. I don't know if that would've been easier or harder. This transition into who-knows-what is confusing. I kind of lost the idea of what I was looking for in the first place ... if I ever truly knew."

"I'm sure you'll work it out. Jesse seems like a reasonable guy. And you've always managed to bounce back."

"Yeah. Thanks. Well, good news, I got my photos into a show here in February. Do you want to come to the opening in a couple weeks?"

"Dan and I are going to the Dominican. We were wondering if you could come and stay at the house. And keep an eye on Olive."

"Sure, I think that could work. It'd be nice to get out of my parents' basement for a while and I can certainly look after your cat."

"Thanks. You'd be doing us a huge favour. I'm looking forward to getting away."

Ж

From: Jesse
To: Maraya
Subject: Can we please make up?

Hello Maraya,

It makes me sad that you and I are not talking. I do not want to cause you any misery, which is why I have stayed "away," why I am not trying to make you "hold on" (still a term I don't like, but nevertheless, the way you are feeling), and I wonder if the day will come when you and I can talk again. I am not happy, and I wish we could hug instead of talk.

Thinking of you often,

/j

From: Maraya
To: Jesse
Subject: Re: Can we please make up?

Dear Jesse,

It's been a long time since you greeted me by my name—it seems strange. You do not cause me misery. Like you said—I cause it to myself. Sometimes I get triggered by things you say and the way you say them. Not by you and your desire to keep in touch with me. Misery is now in the *not* talking, the *not* hugging. My feelings change daily—you should know that by now. They even out quickly. Seems like yours do too. I'm not happy either.

I've been staying at Nicola's while she's in the Dominican with her husband. It's a nice reprieve from my parents' basement, yet makes me feel like I'm still travelling. I'll have some photos in a couple art shows. At least I'm making some mileage with them.

You're on my mind like a lead weight. Thank you for writing. I feel much better now that I know you're not angry with me.

xMx

From: Jesse
To: Maraya
Subject: Re: Can we please make up?

Darling,

I began to think maybe what I wanted between us, what I was trying to "convince" you of, was terribly selfish of me and, in my insensitivity, I was just causing you pain. Even though, yes, we cause ourselves our own pain, it doesn't mean I should ignore that. I know you're somewhat mercurial, but it is those moments when you are miserable that I could be more aware of. So, I thought I should just pull away for a while so you and I could have time to stand back from each other (even though you haven't left my mind or heart for a moment) and I thought that doing so right after we had a fight would maximize the opportunity. It's been a few weeks. That's long enough, right? It has been long enough for me to think about some of my own issues, issues I have deliberately been avoiding, for a long time.

I wasn't angry with you. I was just annoyed that you were "throwing your toys out of the playpen." And even if I was angry with you, I didn't miss you any less. I wanted to have you here, in front of me, so I could yell at you face to face (and then end up hugging). Not being able to hug you is far more upsetting than anything else.

xojox

From Maraya
To: Jesse
Subject: Re: Can we please make up?

And Darling to you too,

That feels so much better. Sad yearning, warm fuzzies, but better to be sharing this way than in anger.

I think it's the jibber jabber, the mundane, that keeps couples going on the day-to-day level. I profess to hate superficial unnecessary stuff but maybe it really is important. It gives a context to our lives. It fills the space that might otherwise remain empty. I'm way too critical and demanding and want intensity all the time. It's not good. I have a fear of boredom. I think it's a fear of death thing—emptiness. As long as something is happening—I feel alive—and that must be good. At least it's entertaining.

I feel alone, you feel alone, we're all here to witness each others' lives—to make them matter. To feel like we matter. That's why we share the trivial, meaningless stuff—as if it matters. You matter. What you're doing, what you're thinking—it matters to me. So, tell me.

When I think of skyping, seeing you, that doesn't feel so good ... because if I see you it just makes it harder to not be feeling you. And that doesn't mean I won't do it. I will.

I'm going to *practica* tonight but let's talk soon.

xMx

When Nicola and Dan returned, she was coughing. It had started before they left. She feared there might be some kind of mould in her home or perhaps she was allergic to her beloved cat. She kept the house clean, used essential oils and had an air purifier going. But, having been in a humid Caribbean climate, and then on a plane, caused the cough to worsen. Because of her compromised immune system, a result of the cancer and the treatment, it was important for her to get it checked out.

Precisely one year after Nicola's initial cancer diagnosis, twenty-one tumours were found in her lungs.

CHAPTER 28

A Bad Trip is Better Than No Trip at All

I woke up with a headache like my head against a board
Twice as cloudy as I'd been the night before
And I went in seeking clarity.

Indigo Girls

To: Jesse
From: Maraya
Subject: Expansion

Dear Jesse,

I have a chance to do a shamanic journey with Ayahuasca here at home so I think I'll go for it. After hearing about it first from you when you were talking to Agnes about her journey, then from a lovely young man I had recently shared a gallery space with, I started to consider it more seriously. The third nudge (I always pay attention when things come in threes)—my brother, Bob, did it last summer and he's still experiencing the effects. He encouraged me to try it. You know I'm not much for playing around with chemicals anymore, but maybe a shamanic journey will provide me with some insight. I'm scared but I'm kind of running out of ideas on how else to proceed.

M

From: Jesse
To: Maraya
Subject: Re: Expansion

Hey,

That's awesome—you should totally do it! Too bad you can't do it in Peru—but it's excellent that you get to do it right where you live. Sounds like it all came together with perfect timing and was meant to be. Don't worry. It'll be fine. I've had several crazy experiences with it and I'm still standing … (barely)

/j

In order to "feed my head," I researched Wikipedia and discovered that an Ayahuasca ceremony would put me in place for a potential "massive spiritual revelation." *Woo hoo, sign me up!* It's touted as "one of the most effective tools of enlightenment." *Perfect.* "It's nearly always said that people experience profound positive changes." *Nearly always? That's pretty good odds.* "Hallucinations and purging negative energy and emotions built up over a life-time was thought to be an essential part of the experience." *Oh,…great….*"Ingestion can cause significant (but temporary) emotional and psychological distress." *I guess that's where the "nearly" comes in.* I had no problem with watching movies in my head but wasn't keen on vomiting. But, time was running short for me to get my shit together. I still felt encumbered and unenlightened, so I was prepared to do things I'd previously said I would never do. I was willing to be flexible in order to transform into someone new and different. I was willing to get stoned.

From: Maraya
To: Bob
Subject: Journeying

Hi Bob,

I paid my deposit for the Healing Circle. What do I tell our mother?

Maraya

From: Bob
To: Maraya
Subject: Re: Journeying

That's great! Tell Mom you're participating in a traditional Peruvian healing ceremony. You don't have to say it involves ingesting psychotropic plants. If you want to tell her, then by all means do so. Heck, Mom and Henry travelled all the way to Brazil to see a healer. I can't see where this would be too weird for her to understand. I've told only a few people but I feel strongly that what I did was of great benefit and of no harm whatsoever. I'm excited for you. You'll be fine. I'm sorry I won't be there to share in the journey. Perhaps some other time. You will have the opportunity for one-on-one healing during the ceremony if there is any physical, emotional or spiritual issue you want tended to. Go with a clear idea of what it is you want. You may not get it but you do get what you deserve, they say. Let go and trust. Let the plant do her work!

Love and Strength,

Bob

I arranged a ride out to the farm just outside of Calgary, where the ceremony was to be held, with someone who had "journeyed" more than thirty times. *Seriously? If the damn thing worked why would he need to keep doing it?* I kept my question to myself. He advised me to make the effort to ensure I got maximum benefit from the experience. I should go get more of the mixture if I didn't feel anything happening. I should go up for hands-on healing to facilitate the process if I didn't feel like enough was happening. I should be brave; no harm would come to me. His words essentially parroted those of my brother. I felt some relief as I entered the outbuilding on the small acreage, calm and ready. There were already two rows of sleeping bags set up side by side against the north and south walls. Some people seemed to know each other and chatted in hushed tones. I squeezed my bag into a prime location closest to the fire—since I was warned I might experience chills—but farthest from the bathroom—a problem should I experience the need to purge.

There were about two dozen participants, each there for an individual journey, so no introductions nor building of rapport was necessary. With the bare minimum said by José, an American shaman and one of the facilitators, the ceremony began. He explained that two psychotropic herbs were combined and brewed on-site. Each of us went up to the altar in turn to receive a small plastic cup with two ounces of a vile "vine of the dead" mixture and returned to our respective sleeping bags. Once each participant had a cup, José said a prayer and together we downed the mixture and settled in, waiting for something to happen. José posed the question for us to answer silently to ourselves: "What is it you seek with the medicine that you do not think you will find without it?"

Anything that could help me get clear about my future was welcome.

I lay down, closed my eyes, and focused on my breath. I lost all sense of time. Nothing was happening. I started to get irritated. I was annoyed with the chanting and I didn't like the music. I wasn't receiving any visions. I observed my irritability, my impatience, my negativity, my judgment—all increasing. I was not in a good space and I didn't want to be there. I reminded myself to surrender, to release my critic. I pushed through my negativity and resistance and heeded all advice—which was rather unlike me. When more medicine was offered—I took more. Still

158

nothing. When healing was offered—I accepted. I was determined to get more out of the experience.

Then, I started to see pictures in my mind: fleeting visions, panoramas of tiny pixelated images—some outlined in black but with multi-coloured interiors, ancient forms, and small snakes. Ephemeral, there was no one distinct image that I could capture, nor remember clearly. I felt like a thousand tiny green scrub brushes (like the toilet bowl cleaner commercial) were inside me cleaning me out. The chanting began to make me smile—it was so silly. If it had been in English it would have sounded childish. In Spanish it sounded much better, holy even: "Ayahuasca: *limpiando, ayudando, arreglando* (cleaning, helping, fixing), open the heart, open the eyes, each one, everyone, *cada uno, todo*."

Again, my negative judgment reared up. I had entered into this experience open, calm, positive and accepting and, in no time, I'd turned into a horrible critic. I wanted the whole thing to end. I was physically uncomfortable: my back hurt, my Therm-a-Rest wouldn't hold enough air, and I was cold. Then, without much warning, I started retching into the empty yogourt container beside me. Fortunately, I had complied with the suggestion to fast. Afterward, the taste in my mouth was unusually sweet and minty and a voice in my head said, "Your friend told you it would be like this," and I had a "memory" that this was so. Later I questioned that "memory." I think I had made it all up. No real person had told me any such thing. I yawned deeply, repeatedly, and my eyes were leaking. I must have slept because I returned to some level of consciousness with a jolt when I heard drumming and music I liked. I realized I'd been crying. I didn't stop for a very long time.

The "jolt" I experienced was about my younger brother, Jay. The message I got was that he would be "transitioning" soon. The message wasn't straightforward, it wasn't so succinct, but that was the essence of it. That was what I understood. In my hallucination, Jay asked for forgiveness. I don't know what for. I forgave him. I apologized for being a lousy big sister. Since there were ten years between us, I had missed out a lot on his life while he was growing up; I didn't know him and he didn't know me. Who had pushed whom away? I don't know how much was spirit and how much was ego—those voices in my head. The crying continued anew each time I renewed the thought of loss. I grieved for a lost relationship, one that never was. I ached with sadness. I got chills and tried to snuggle deeper into my sleeping bag. Maybe I needed to forgive myself.

The situation didn't relate to what I had asked for clarity about. It was a tangent taking me off my path—like what had happened so many times in the past. Supposedly, the "entities" at these ceremonies knew more than us and what we needed than we did. It's out of our conscious control. We don't always get what we want. *Do we get what we need?*

I felt the urge to pee all the time, but it was such an effort to go to the bathroom and it didn't seem to help anyway. Eventually, the room got quiet, except for light snoring, and I relaxed into a deep dreamless sleep.

I must've been the last to wake up in the morning just in time to share briefly. We went around the group and each person spoke. I expressed that the experience had been unpleasant in so many ways. I didn't feel "light" or "cleansed." I felt sad. I felt slightly stronger, maybe calmer, maybe clearer, after purging. I had asked for clarity and maybe I would only get to see ten feet in front of me, not ten miles; one day at a time, not a whole year. We shared a potluck breakfast and I caught a ride back to the city with a couple of participants. We engaged in small talk but mostly we drove back in silence, each still processing our own personal experience.

Back at my parents' place, my temporary home, I looked forward to a quiet contemplative weekend by myself to process my experience before my trip to Mexico. The rest of the family planned to go to Edmonton to spend time with my brother Jay and his wife before they returned to her native Switzerland. I had not wanted to join them but now felt compelled to go. According to my hallucinations, Jay's "transition" might mean more than just returning to Europe. And, if I believed the drug-induced prophecy, I might never see him again.

Ж

It was a bloody cold day in the city of my birth and early childhood. A dense curtain of snow fell softly as we drove toward the center of Edmonton. It obscured the view of the downtown core across the North Saskatchewan River from Skunk Hollow. Most of the family was meeting, maybe for the last time (as my mother felt the need to say more and more as she grew older), at least for the last time before my brother and his wife left the country.

It was always good to see my family, we got along swell—we never fought. We tend not to appreciate a lot of small talk and I felt I had little of consequence to say to my little brother. If there was something he needed to say to me, I was there, open and receptive. Maybe we could just enjoy our time together … until next time.

While I watched Bohemian Waxwings nosh on clumps of red Rowan berries hanging from skeleton trees in the small forest outside the side window of the small home, I contemplated the fragility and fleeting temporariness of life and the ties that bind us. How fortunate I've been to have the family I have.

CHAPTER 29
Move as You Feel Guided

I had an urge to drive La Ruta Maya before the end of the Mayan calendar in 2012—just in case. A psychic once told me I'd been a Mayan shaman in a previous life and that I would find my people—perhaps ghosts of distant ancestors, perhaps kindred spirits—among the stones of the Mayan ruins and in the nearby villages. If I found my people, maybe I would feel a sense of connection. Maybe, among old stones, I would find stillness and solace. I would at least enjoy the ancient art and architecture; I'd always liked rocks.

My octogenarian friend, Bill, and I spent more than five weeks driving from Mexico's west coast to the east coast, then down through Belize and Guatemala and back up again to San Miguel in central Mexico. I enjoyed the road trip, but did not find my spiritual home nor any kindred spirits along the way.

By the time I'd returned to Calgary, Nicola's lower lungs had collapsed, her breathing was belaboured, and she was in a lot of pain. She was at home on oxygen. Her body was riddled with tiny tumours.

She called me for a favour. Troy, a spiritual healer she'd known a long time, was in town and wanted to do a healing session with her. He had no car so Nicola asked if I would pick him up and bring him to her house. I agreed. That way, I would get to see both Troy and her, even if we weren't able to have much of a visit.

When we arrived, Nicola was on the couch, attached to her ventilator, and didn't even get up to greet us. As Troy helped her into the treatment room, Nicola and I exchanged a pained look that spoke of our disappointment with not having more time together—not that day—not ever.

I felt restless. Fleeing back to Buenos Aires before I'd initially intended wouldn't solve my problems—real or imagined—and was more likely to create new ones. The idea to run again was percolating and it nudged me out from underneath flannel sheets where I had sequestered myself in the middle of the day to incubate my un-namable despair. I rose to investigate the possibility of escape.

Why don't you just go for two weeks? coaxed a voice inside my head.

I hadn't considered that as a possibility. It didn't seem financially wise. Should I leave pronto for a short burst and return to see out the summer or could I hang on at home until winter loomed and then fly south? Both were imperfect options. A two-week "visit" seemed like a band-aid solution to a wound reopened and losing blood. It was spontaneous, it was rash, it was the best damn fix I could think of.

"You've gotta come for at least a month to make it worthwhile," Jesse said over Skype.

"You're probably right. Okay. Are you sure it's okay to stay with you for that long?"

"Sure, no problem. I've got room in my new place."

Some time during the two-week preparation period, I realized it didn't make sense to go for a month, come back for the summer, and then go again in the fall. I didn't have any plans for the summer. *I should just go for a year.* By the time I'd bought a ticket with a one-month return date, I was half convinced I

163

would be staying for a year. I didn't want to admit it to myself and I didn't want to tell anyone. I packed an extra bag to leave at home on "stand-by" in case I stayed; I could have a travelling *tanguero* bring it to me or have it shipped.

A few days after my decision to return for a "visit," Jesse called to tell me he was on his way to the hospital with the old familiar pain in his chest. This sent me for a loop. I needed to talk to someone about my distress. I called Nicola and she said, "I'm not the right person to talk to about this right now. I'm on my way to the hospital for a blood transfusion. I'll call you when I get home."

When it was Dan's voice I heard on the other end of the phone Monday morning over a week later, I knew it was over. Nicola had spent the whole week in the hospital and never returned home. She hadn't wanted anyone to see her while she was there. There would be no funeral, there would be no burial, no memorial was planned, just a BBQ for close friends and family when Dan felt ready. Just like that—it was over, no goodbye.

Three days later, I left for Buenos Aires where I would just have to grieve and heal—again.

Nicola was my last connection to the past, except for my family. We had not always been close, but we'd stayed connected. We'd grown along parallel tracks in the same direction. She had been my oldest and dearest friend, my soul sister.

Nicola had worked hard to get herself to a place where she could help others with her wisdom and guidance. I grieved for my shattered beliefs because of the injustice of her illness and her early death. It didn't seem to make a difference that she had done the right things: lived well, held positive thoughts, ate healthy food, and helped others. I couldn't come to terms with what had happened; cause and effect don't always make sense. *What a fucking loss and disservice to the planet. What kind of a god could be so near-sighted?*

164

From Nicola's blog:

Some would say that all the effort has failed. The cancer is still in my body, therefore none of it worked. But that suggests the definition of healing is a complete reversal of the situation. This point of view fails to see that healing can be defined in many ways. Through my healing journey, I have healed relationships, deep emotional trauma, limiting core beliefs, and evolved spiritually so very much in just 50 years.

We humans think we are in control of everything, but what we often fail to acknowledge is our life's plan, or our soul's path if you want to call it that. Our lack of spiritual connection makes us fear death and see it as some terrible tragedy instead of a natural part of life that is simply a transition from one state of being to another.

I accept that it may be part of my life's plan to transition from this life sooner rather than later. I'm also pursuing healing because I feel it's never too late or too hopeless to heal. I'm doing my best to listen to spirit and to allow myself to be guided. I only do what I feel moved to do now. Perhaps it required a diagnosis of terminal cancer to finally get me to live this way.

CHAPTER 30

On the Edge of the Big Ditch

Buenos Aires gets under your skin, into your veins, and rattles your bones. I needed a transfusion. I arrived the last Friday in May. Jesse was not on the corner near his new apartment on Calle Defensa as agreed. The *taxista* and I were trying to figure out what to do, because the street was inaccessible to vehicle traffic, when Jesse walked up the sidewalk with bags of groceries.

We embraced awkwardly. "Hey," he said, and kissed me.

"Hey."

"Good to see you. How was your flight?"

"Long."

"I got us some food."

"I'm not that hungry. I just feel like cuddling, if that's okay with you."

"Sure, sounds good. We can eat later."

We took the stairs up to the first floor of the old converted *conventillo*. Jesse's apartment shared a landing with the office of Galería Edea where I'd had my photo exhibition the previous August. "You ever see Brenda?" I asked.

"Nah, she doesn't use that door." He unlocked his door. "Come on in. Kick your shoes off."

The apartment was so much bigger than his previous studio. "Wow. Nice space."

"Yeah, I like it. You can just put your stuff there." He pointed to a daybed in the large entryway. "I'm thinking of turning this area into a bedroom and getting a roommate. Wasted space otherwise, and I could use the money."

The kitchen was tiny, adequate for Jesse, but the front room was huge. He had set part of it up as an office. I went to the open window and leaned out. "Amazing. You're right on Defensa. That's so cool. What's it like on Sundays?"

"Noisy."

The San Telmo street fair filled Calle Defensa for several blocks from Calle Belgrano to Plaza Dorrego every Sunday. "I bet. I'm looking forward to being in the middle of the action … at least once."

"Listen, I gotta make some calls. Why don't you settle in and rest, then we'll make dinner and maybe go for a walk or watch a movie."

"Sure. Maybe I'll have a shower too." I left him to his work and busied myself getting acquainted with my new home base.

After dinner, we strolled up Defensa and got ice cream at Freddo's. It felt good to be back in the warm, humid evening air, hanging out with Jesse; it felt comfortable. He got back to work when we returned to the apartment and, exhausted, I hit the sack.

Without skipping a beat, we fell into our old routine the next day. Saturday started mid-afternoon with a tango class with Lucia and Angus. We took the *subte* to Niño Bien. There were quite a few beginners so we didn't learn much that was new to us, but it was our first time dancing together in several months and it felt good. Jesse's dancing had improved over the months but his repertoire hadn't increased much. We stayed just long enough afterward for me to say "Hi" to Cherie and catch up before we headed back to Jesse's where we met with some of his friends at the bar across the street. They wanted to move the party to Jesse's but I vetoed it since my stuff was all over the place and there was nowhere to put my things away securely. Jesse didn't care about the mess but he respected the fact that I cared about my belongings.

So, we went home early and eagerly. But the sex didn't go so well. He couldn't follow through. Health issues and medications had taken their toll.

"That's okay," I said. "You'll get this heart situation sorted out eventually and you'll be back to your old self."

"Yeah, maybe," he grumbled and turned to the wall.

I awoke in the night to a throng of words fighting to escape the confines of my head. Two internal channels were playing simultaneously: A music channel was on endless replay of Jacques Brel's *Ne Me Quitte Pas* and, since I didn't know Jesse's favourite French version, I silently sang it in English and began to translate it into Spanish. *If you go away* … The other channel broadcasted a story, clamouring to be heard.

It had always been easy for me to shun the muse when she arrived in the middle of the night, especially when … well, really, anytime and all the time—since my favourite place for refuge was between the sheets with my lover, who, in this case, was warm beside me after such a long time. Yet, for the first time in so long, I felt an urge to rise and write, and I answered it.

I went into the living room with my laptop and started pounding out what I knew about the building I was in, and what it wanted to tell me. The apartment had so much history, it was rife with stuck energy. *Ghosts?* It had been a tenement house, one of hundreds in the San Telmo *barrio*. Nuns had nursed those dying of cholera in the 1800s in this very space. Jesse thought they still haunted the anteroom. He said computers never worked in there; the nuns didn't appreciate technology.

El Zanjón de Granados was right next door. It had been built in the 1830s as a luxury mansion and abandoned in the 1870s because of the yellow fever epidemic. It was divided into tenements and later abandoned and basically just used as a dump.

168

Jorge Eckstein purchased the property in 1985 with a dream of opening a restaurant and an art gallery. The garbage had been piled up higher than the front door on the main level from the deterioration and settling of debris. When the floor collapsed, it revealed an original underground cistern. Further exploration revealed tunnels and caverns. Imagine having to remove over 1,000 tonnes of other people's trash from your basement.

Two blocks away, Avenida Paseo de Colon was once the shore of the Rio de la Plata. The river has receded by about three kilometres over the years. Underground channels and open sewers were the source of cholera and yellow fever. Wealthy San Telmo inhabitants moved to Recoleta but the poor remained and many died. The channels were bricked up and built over top of. Grand homes of the wealthy became *conventillos* to accommodate the less fortunate.

El Zanjón took almost 20 years to restore and was opened to the public in 2003. Although an important historical site, the Zanjón de Granados project received no government funds. Perhaps it was politically unwise for Mayor Macri to throw money into the "big ditch." Since no money has been spent on excavating and exploring other tunnels in the area, it's hard to know what else lies beneath the cobblestones of San Telmo.

There are ghosts in the walls and there is an uneasiness in the street as dawn lights up the fact that it's time to end the party and return home to sleep most of Sunday away. The day crew will soon secure locations for vendors as the street closes to vehicle traffic and opens to pedestrians. I went back to bed, hoping to get a couple hours of sleep before Jesse woke up.

Going for brunch Sunday mornings was one of our favourite things to do together, but Jesse ended up on the phone most of the morning ... and then the afternoon. He talked to everyone else he also hadn't seen for ages—while the San Telmo Street Fair raged below the open window. And, there I was in the

169

flesh…invisible to him. Something was off. I headed out to walk the distance of the frenzied fair alone.

Monday, I barely made it to yoga, but not before some asshole grabbed my wrist, as I was walked down Calle Florida, so that I couldn't return whatever it was that had fallen out of the pocket of the man walking in front of me. This happened the split second a nearby woman stumbled onto her face and people were approaching her to help. I guess it smelled like one of the many street scams perpetrated in the inner city. Maybe it was. Yoga helped me shift my shitty mood a smidgen.

Jesse had implemented his version of our respective tango dreams to have an alternative *milonga* at Independéncia 572, where we'd danced before. It was only a few blocks from his apartment. He couldn't secure Friday nights so decided to start with Mondays. Not a great choice of nights for a *milonga*, but it would give him time to get his entrepreneurial feet wet and make a name for himself in the tango community.

He took a nap before heading over to set up for the *milonga* while I cooked dinner. As soon as he got to the venue, he called me. "Hey, my waitress didn't show up. Do you think you can help out?"

The closest I'd ever been to waiting tables was as an A&W car hop in the early '70s. And, those weren't tables; they were cars. *Wait tables at a milonga in Buenos Aires? That definitely sounds like something worth writing home about....* "Uh,...I'm not sure I can pull that off. I'm not comfortable enough with my Spanish—I might screw up."

"Don't worry about it. Your Spanish is good enough for the basics of table-waiting."

"Well, let's see how it goes—okay? I'll pick up the slack by bussing and washing dishes. Maybe it won't be busy and Lucia can handle the waitressing. If not, then I guess I can give it a try."

170

Since it was a new *milonga* on a Monday night, it wasn't busy at all and Lucia handled it. I helped in the back behind the scenes. Jesse and I danced on an empty floor. His energy was declining again—much like the previous time we'd been in that same venue. At the end of the night, Lucia cooked up a big pot of pasta for the staff and we enjoyed a late meal together.

I'd been back a week and had the distinct feeling things had changed between us, but I hadn't received the memo. There was tension and I didn't know why. I knew Jesse's health weighed on him and he partly addressed that by medicating with street drugs and booze. He was concerned about the viability of the *milonga*; finances, like always, were a real concern. We fought, or I just shut down, not engaging with his pissy mood.

Jesse had agreed to let me stay for a month, but maybe that was too much commitment for him. He didn't yet know I had come with the consideration of staying longer. Now that I was back, I knew I wanted to stay for a year. I would have to tell him and see how he felt about me staying with him for that length of time.

We walked up Defensa and went into a tiny cafe for hot chocolate.

"I'm thinking of staying longer than a month," I said tentatively as we sat down.

"Oh yeah?"

"Yeah.... Rather than leave and come back again in the fall like I'd planned, I thought I'd just stay for a year or so."

He shifted in his seat, looking a little uncomfortable, but remained silent.

"What do you think of me staying with you for the duration?"

"No, I don't think that's going to work," he blurted without hesitation.

"No, I suppose not...."

I don't know what I'd been thinking. Hopeful, I guess. Unrealistic. That would be far too much closeness and commitment for him. Probably for me too. He stayed freaked out for a few days. I had changed the tone of our visit way too soon. Rather than enjoy our time together, I would have find another place to live as soon as possible.

Eventually, Jesse calmed down and we were able to talk rationally about his fears and me overstepping my boundaries. A conversation eased some of the tension and we relaxed. We drank some wine, and he smoked and did a few lines. Both feeling good, we locked onto each other like old times, but it became too much exertion for Jesse and he had to stop in excruciating pain. He fumbled around for a couple nitro tabs, upset that he couldn't perform. "Coke makes me feel like I can do whatever I want…but my body doesn't always comply," he said.

"No worries," I said, hoping to reassure him.

Again, he was embarrassed—believing I only got to see the worst of him.

Ж

I'd only been back in Buenos Aires about three weeks and my lungs were working vigorously to expel the accumulated toxic build-up. The cough was different from Calgary's dry-climate throat cough. I felt pressure in my lungs. Coughing in order to expectorate is a good…unless it's an indication of a deeper problem….

"What's with all the coughing?" Jesse asked. "I'm the smoker —and not exhaling in your direction. You're coughing more than I am."

"I think it started in Guatemala after I shared a huge doobie with Anna. She and Enrique smoke two of those mothers a day.

She says they're big because the weed is poor quality. I guess my near-virgin lungs were offended."

"You probably have pot fungus then. You should go get it checked out."

"Yeah, right. 'Hey Doc—I got pot fungus smoking a doobie in Guatemala. Can you give me something for it?' That'll go over real well."

"You don't have to tell him anything. Just get it checked out. Maybe you can get it cleared up with antibiotics."

"No. You know how I feel about the medical industry. I'll just keep an eye on it. My lungs are getting used to the pollution here all over again. Once I've purged the car exhaust I'll be fine. I have a strong immune system."

"Famous last words. Didn't you just have a friend die of lung cancer?"

"Two of them, actually."

"Two? Shit. Seriously? You didn't tell me about the other one."

"He wasn't a smoker either ... well, except for pot. He wasn't a close friend, just a neighbour I hung out with once in a while. I visited him in the hospital the day Gerry died. Cancer started in his lungs, went into his bones, then his brain; he went really fast."

"Man, people drop off around you like flies."

"Yeah, you better watch yourself...."

CHAPTER 31

After Nirvana … Then What?

My country is the tango and its capital is Corrientes Street.

Carlos Gardel

After a tense month at Jesse's, I moved back to Corrientes Street, only two blocks away from *el Obelisco*. The apartment was on the second floor facing the street, in a beautiful old-fashioned building, complete with maid's quarters off the kitchen where I set up a little "office." The location made it far more convenient to get to my favourite dance venues. I was around the corner from the South American Explorers office where I could drop in for Spanish classes or walk a few blocks farther up Lavalle to Vero's for tutoring. It was a hop, skip and a jump to Escuela Argentino de Tango and a short *subte* ride to Estudio DNI's new location. It was good to have my own place again.

No one had rented the second bedroom so I had the whole apartment to myself. I did, however, have to clean it first—it was pretty disgusting, especially the bath tub. And I had to purchase my own linens. Luckily, an expat was moving onto a boat so I bought all kinds of things I needed from her, and many things I didn't.

The Swine Flu followed me to Buenos Aires. I had escaped Mexico the day after they'd closed the schools. I arrived in Canada and incubated for two weeks. Nothing. Here, fear of *el gripe* gripped the population. People, should they venture out into public, covered their faces with surgical masks or winter scarves. Schools were closing and *milongas* were either cancelled or suffered from lack of patronage. We started just making kissy noises near cheeks without contact when we greeted each other, and people stopped sharing *mate* with strangers. Friends still shared with each other but, overall, the exchange of body fluids was curtailed.

Julio arrived at *practica* wearing a surgical mask. Since Julio was in his seventies, he took his mortality, and protection of his health, more seriously than most of the dancers at Estudio DNI. I didn't repeat what the Home Care Nurse had told me—that the masks are virtually useless as a form of protection against others. I did suggest that handwashing was the most effective way to prevent the spread of disease, especially important behaviour in a public situation where many people are dancing with each other. Julio took me aside and in a lowered tone confided to me that most men do not wash their hands before leaving the restroom. Too much information.

I spent the rest of the day at DNI dancing with the brave souls unafraid of infection. The young *porteño* I was dancing with asked if it was my first time there.

"*No, vos?*"

"*Si.*"

He lived in the countryside. He was tall, handsome, and dressed in black. He didn't practice the pattern we had just been shown. He seemed to feel the music deeply and expressed it spontaneously and exquisitely with his movement. I stopped expecting to do what we'd been told; I didn't care. For those few moments, I closed my eyes and just felt; I surrendered. It didn't matter how old he was; I was in love. His feeling for the tango was more than I had ever felt before; dancing with him was the ultimate tango sensation. I had reached Nirvana. I wanted more of him and yet, after class when he asked me to dance, I was already halfway out the door, late for an appointment.

Maipu 444 was a short walk from my apartment. I was to meet Linda and Juan Carlos, a taxi dancer. Linda had met him in a class, in which he'd assisted, and hired him to attend a *milonga* with her. Dancing every *tanda* with him had been exhausting, so sharing him with another dancer seemed like a better idea. I was happy to be included.

The entrance to the venue was nondescript. I walked up the long, narrow wooden staircase from the street to a small landing with a heavy curtain. As the curtain parted, all eyes looked to see who had just arrived. It was so intimidating.

The DJ was the same as the one from Niño Bien on Saturdays. So, the music, as usual, bored me after a couple of *tandas*. But, the dancing didn't. Juan Carlos was close to my size and slim, and a superb lead. Sitting out left me available to dance with others but, if people know you're with a taxi dancer, they are reluctant to ask; I only danced with him. Dancing only every second *tanda* with him may have been enough for Linda, but it wasn't enough for me.

Unfortunately, our paid-for time was cut short because they decided to close the venue early since most of the dancers had left. I wanted more.

Ж

Because of the "pandemic," some 4th of July events were cancelled, but there was still a lot going on. I got in touch with Linda to see what she was up to. We decided to check out a few options. After a bite to eat, Linda, her friend Sandra, and I headed to Niño Bien to be greeted by a half-full room of die-hard *milongueros*. We endured the *milonga* etiquette with the limited opportunities and, after dancing a couple of *tandas,* decided to head off to the first in a string of 4th of July parties. Meanwhile, our own energy levels were questionable as we succumbed to the semi-pervasive feeling of infirmity developing within the population. Everyone seemed to fear the worst; dark, dismal energy tends to feed on itself.

We did not feel in the mood to take the bus. Three to a cab across town seemed more efficient and affordable. We arrived at a speakeasy in someone's apartment to be greeted by only the host, dressed in shorts and sandals. He said he hadn't expected anyone to show up—and they hadn't. We stayed long enough to chat with the tropical birds, inhale more of the gas leak and, by this time, discouraged and thinking it too early to arrive at the next party, considered calling it a night.

My *compañeras* headed one way and I hopped into a cab to go home. The young *taxista* asked me the usual, personal questions: was I here alone; did I have a boyfriend; do I like Buenos Aires?

I told him I had a *novio.* "No, he's not Argentine."

"*Bueno,*" he said, "you should be careful with *los Argentinos.*"

As I was leaving the cab, he asked me out for a drink. I noticed how attractive he was—and about twenty years younger than me. *Damn!* I smiled sweetly and reminded him I had a boyfriend.

He said, "He's not invited."

I reinforced my NO. *Never say yes to a man you haven't at least seen standing up.*

With a lighter bounce in my step, I returned to my apartment and phoned my *novio,*

"How was your night?" Jesse asked.

"It ended better than it started," I said, smiling to myself.

"Well, that sounds intriguing. Want to tell me about it?"

"Nope. I'm good. I just want to turn in."

"Okay, well, sweet dreams then, see you tomorrow."

CHAPTER 32
Love, or Something Like It

We are verses out of rhythm, couplets out of rhyme.

Paul Simon, *The Dangling Conversation*

The next Saturday, we had our usual class with Lucia and Angus and Jesse came back to my place for a change. Now that the pressure of living together was off, and we had some distance, our relationship had improved. It was almost like it had been before I'd left for Christmas.

Sundays had always been my favourite part of our relationship. Jesse always wanted to get up and go for a smoke and a coffee right away but I savoured the lingering, the possibility of making love, the intimate conversation. I tried to stretch it out as long as I could. Once we went out for brunch, we would continue the dialogue and by mid afternoon we would part and I hated that transition. If we stayed in bed it continued to feel like the beginning.

We hadn't had a lengthy serious conversation since I'd returned. There was something I needed to know. Something that was evident by its absence and I always feared asking the difficult questions. With him it was easier. He was more likely to engage in difficult conversations with me than most men I knew, as long as he was in the mood. I just came right out and asked, "Why don't you love me?"

"I don't know," he replied, unfazed by my directness.

"That's a lame answer. You're just trying to avoid the difficult question. You used to love me—at least you used to say it."

"When I said it, I meant it."

"What happened? I don't sense your feelings have diminished at all...except for when we're fighting ... or living together, of course."

He started to appear pained by my confrontation but he pushed through it. "What happened was, I realized I was heading down the same road I'd been down before. That journey caused me heartache, repeatedly, and I decided to pull back."

"So, you got scared." I turned away and smoothed out the sheets around me.

"No," he said, sitting up and adjusting his pillow. "I just decided I'm not going there. Love is a stupid word. It doesn't mean anything. I don't know what it means. Nobody seems to agree on what it means. So, it just loses its meaning."

"Well, on one hand it's loaded with meaning—but I agree. We have to decide for ourselves what it means to us. That's why we have a conversation about it. Two people should get a little clearer on it together. This special 'thing' between two people usually smacks of commitment and responsibility and sometimes manipulation."

I continued—on a roll with my monologue while he got up, opened the window, and lit a cigar. "I feel insecure in this relationship. I feel insecure for so many reasons and I've never felt quite like this in a relationship before. Maybe it's my age. I don't know. It's whittling away at my self-esteem. First, because I never knew if you would live from one day to the next—afraid you might die on top of me while we were having sex. Sometimes I felt like I just wanted you to die and get it over with so I could heal from that drama and be done. But it went on and on for a while and now you seem to be on an even slower road to self-destruction and doom so I have to deal with our eventual separation instead as I come to love you more and more and, in any moment, you could just go up in smoke." I punctuated my words with a dramatic hand gesture and continued. "You keep reminding me you don't want a relationship, all the while saying we are indeed having a relationship—but that you are just not willing to make any promises—about exclusivity or permanence. There's no security and I feel insecure."

"Did you feel secure in your other relationships?"

"Well," I pondered, "... good question. I suppose, at times I did because we had agreements—we had a commitment and we spoke of love; we worked together toward a common future. And, look what happened there." I rolled my eyes and threw up my hands in defeat.

"Nothing is for certain," I surmised and Jesse nodded in agreement.

"Nothing can truly be promised," he said. "There's no security whether we speak of it or we don't."

While I tried to wrap my mind around that, I continued. "So, basically you're saying you're not willing to speak of it—but just to engage in it in the moment—and that frankly, our moment—our moments—are pretty damn good."

"Exactly. And as far as I'm concerned, it's the action in the moment that matters."

"Right. Falling in love is completely different from loving someone. Choosing to love someone and treating them well through your intent, your words and your actions is what matters. Still, that needy romantic place in me wants to hear those words from you—from my special man of the moment."

"But it doesn't mean anything," he insisted.

I shifted. "It *does* mean something or you wouldn't have such a hard time with it. You've got loads of baggage attached to it and

NOT saying it takes up a bunch of energy that you don't even notice. You should practice saying it over and over until it loses its charge for you. Then it will truly lose whatever meaning you've attached to it and you can reframe it. Use it like a game 'I love you, pass the sugar; I'm wiping my ass because I love you,' or whatever. Your history with it is controlling you. You think by not dealing with it directly, it'll just go away. But there's always another person involved—whether it's love or non-love, and so here we are revealing the elephant in the room—why you won't say what you used to say that represented or represents what you feel or used to feel." I paused so he could process that. "Use more appropriate language—say what you mean. That's the trick. Like…during love-making: 'I so enjoy sharing pleasurable times with you.'" I giggled.

"I do. I told you I was thinking of you with great fondness last week."

"Yuck. I take issue with the word 'fondness.' I want more than that. We don't have a future—I know that—no long-term type of commitment, but we have a certain amount of time together and I'd like to feel more secure. Somehow, I guess I just want you to state the obvious."

"Well if it's obvious I shouldn't have to state it."

"I hate it when you're so fucking rational. You make me crazy—I hate you!" I bashed him with a pillow.

"See what I mean? That's so fucked up. That's my point. You hate me and you love me. It makes no sense."

"It makes sense to me. It's a paradox. I have intense feelings for you, damn it!"

"That's better. I have feelings for you too."

"Well, right now, I hate you," I said with pouty lips.

He grabbed me around the waist. I started tickling him in defense.

"Stop that—don't tickle me."

"Or else what?"

He threw me down onto the bed, pinned me with his body and kissed me deeply. "You think too much, dear."

"I know. That's why I need somebody to fuck me senseless on a regular basis."

"Happy to oblige."

We continued our conversation at breakfast. "I just can't get used to constantly trying to live in the present," I said as a way to get us back into the dialogue. "We all tend to want to cling to some kind of certainty, to believe something real and permanent exists for us. Our addiction to hope is good—it keeps us moving forward. Sitting with the constant anxiety of uncertainty is difficult for me. I would prefer to be distracted. I still grieve the past; I still worry about the future. I'm having such a hard time enjoying the present."

His mouth was full so I continued. "Tango, more than any other dance, and especially for the man, or the one who leads, is the best way I know to maintain the present. But, unfortunately, we can't dance all the time. We have to dwell in and deal with the reality we've created. Chop wood, carry water; one foot in front of the other—baby steps."

"Like I've told you before, I share more with you than I do anybody," he managed to squeeze in between bites. "I feel more comfortable with you, closer to you, than anybody. This is the healthiest relationship I've ever had."

I was on a roll. "Yes, and it *is* a relationship. It always was and, as long as we're relating, it always will be. Quit telling me you don't want a relationship because for so many reasons you do—and it's just the parameters of it you need to establish. You don't want to lose your freedom as you perceive it—but it's up to you to stand your ground there. I can't take anything away from you. No one can take your freedom. You're good at setting your boundaries and maintaining them—especially with me. But don't get mad at me when you lose your boundaries around me—it's not my fault.

"We also, at this point, do not have any spoken agreement about exclusivity or not," I continued, "and that could be a bit of a problem. But I expect we'll tell each other if we're doing anything that could potentially affect the physical or emotional health of the other."

"Yup, that's for sure. I'll have no problem telling you what I've got going on—when I've got it going on."

At least that felt like some kind of agreement. Yet, I wondered if I asked for too much.

CHAPTER 33
Day Trip to Colonia

Since I hadn't quite planned to stay in Buenos Aires a year when I'd left Calgary, I hadn't packed my hiking boots, not knowing I would need them for my trip to Patagonia. The only decent footwear I had was my Birkenstocks; they wouldn't work for hiking.

I resisted buying something I already owned, albeit at home in Canada, so I looked around for several weeks until I finally found the perfect compromise: not a runner (have those), not a hiking boot (have those) but a hiking *shoe*. I tried them on in my suspected size but they were a tad roomy in the toes—not much of a problem especially after I'd suffered the discomfort of pointy boots for the past three months. I didn't have my credit card with me so intended to return the following week to purchase them.

When I returned to the store, I thought I'd try on a half size smaller if they were available. Even a whole size smaller might work better.

"Do you have these in 7½?"

The salesman went to the backroom to check and I sat down to wait. He came out, walked past me to the desk where he pulled one shoe out of the box and brought it to me. It was the wrong shoe.

"I only have it in this colour," he said and walked back to the desk.

I sat there, NOT trying it on. I didn't want them in brown. He returned and asked me how it fit. I told him I didn't want that colour. "Do you have the blue one in size 8 or even in size 7?"

He sauntered into the backroom, returned with one box, walked past me to the desk, and brought me one shoe. It was blue, size 6½.

Seriously? "That's too small, do you have a size 8?"

He returned to the backroom, returned with one box, walked past me to the desk, and returned to me with one shoe. I tried on the size 8 while he went to the sales desk to answer the phone and ring up a sale—even though there were several other staff members milling about. I waited. He looked over and I nodded. He brought over the other shoe so I now had an entire pair. That way I could actually walk, not hobble, around the store to determine how they felt.

Just to be sure, I confirmed with him, "So, you have this shoe in size 8, and in size 6½, but not in size 7 or size 7½. Is that correct?"

"Yes."

He disappeared while I walked about. The heels fit snugly, the toes offered plenty of wiggle room. I figured it was the best I could do; I was tired of looking and I had set a long-overdue goal to have proper walking shoes before I explored Colonia, and by the time I went hiking in Patagonia. I went to the sales desk with my intended purchase and pulled out my Visa card and ID. As I waited, my salesclerk reappeared from the backroom. He had, in his hands, exactly the shoe I had asked for twenty minutes earlier. *What a surprise....*I tried on the size 7½ and they fit perfectly.

I'm not sure if there was some hidden sales agenda, a secret retail tactic, to have a customer try on all the wrong sizes and colours before the shoe originally asked for magically appears.

Maybe this is the way we are taught to appreciate our purchases so much more. I doubt it.

Ж

I was nearing the end of my 90-day visa. The government had raised the penalty for overstaying one's welcome from 50 pesos to 300 pesos. I guess they realized they could make money off our bad behaviour. A day trip to Uruguay was the least expensive and least time-consuming solution.

I booked the Colonia Express day trip online for only 129 pesos. It included a one-hour guided walking tour and lunch, which I thought I would just ignore, explore on my own, and then hunker down somewhere with a book. I didn't relish the thought of making the trip and I certainly didn't relish the thought of rising early enough to be at the Ferry Terminal before 7:00 a.m. But, it turned out to be easy to get there earlier than necessary. And, a good thing, since, after I waited 15 minutes for the *Buquebus* information desk to open, I found out the Colonia Express was not operated by *Buquebus,* so I had to take another taxi to the opposite end of Puerto Madero—not an easy feat at 6:45 a.m. Luckily, I had the help of a couple of nice police officers who flagged down a cab for me and, even then, I still arrived earlier than was necessary to the terminal and was quickly processed.

I arrived in Colonia on a holiday—the anniversary of the Independence of Uruguay in 1828. Founded in 1680 by Portugal, Colonia is the oldest town in Uruguay with a population of about 22,000. Evidence that it was passed back and forth between Portugal and Spain several times is expressed in the original architecture and street design of the *Barrio Histórico*—now a UNESCO World Heritage Site. Portuguese cobblestone streets allow for water drainage down the middle and Spanish cobblestone streets allow for drainage down either side.

186

Portuguese homes have sloped, clay-tiled roofs and Spanish roofs are flat.

There's very little to do in this sleepy little town—which made it a welcome change from Buenos Aires. With the holiday, many businesses were closed and there were not a lot of choices of restaurants for lunch. The prices were like they are in most tourist towns—expensive. So, I decided it best to use the voucher included with my ticket. Sometimes being *sola* allows one to be seated quickly in a jam-packed restaurant. I had a perfect spot on the covered sidewalk patio. It was a glorious, sunny, early spring day, and I had a corner from which to enjoy a leisurely meal and watch the families stroll down the street.

I was allowed three choices; I elected to try *chavito*—a dish common to Uruguay. Except for the fact that the bread was the side, it was the best example of bad food combining I had ever seen in my life all heaped up on one plate. Although I'd asked them to leave the ham and bacon off my steak, I had to remove them myself. I dug into the cheese-covered piece of thinly sliced *lomo* and ate the fried egg separately with the French fries. There was a peculiar mix of diced and boiled potatoes, carrots and some kind of pickle, shredded lettuce, and tomato. It was a super-sized full-meal deal.

I enjoyed a pleasant stroll through the old historic area, sat in the sun and wrote, and was in a blissful state by the time I got onto the ferry to return to Argentina.

CHAPTER 34

Rising Above

Compared to the Tango, the Blues are just a colour.

The situation between Jesse and me continued to deteriorate. He was either busy with work or the *milonga* or he seemed distracted. He was drinking heavily, doing a lot of drugs, and hanging around with some shady characters. He was quick to anger; he complained of pain and fatigue; he just wasn't fun to be around. I busied myself with tango and Spanish classes, and expat events. We were free to see whomever we wanted, and I felt ready to pursue a "real" relationship but, although I'd made lots of friends, I hadn't met anyone I was interested in pursuing. I didn't *need* him,...still,...I missed him.

I had to move from Corrientes Street because the owner had just decided to sell, or, at least, had just decided to tell me they were selling. Finding new places to live wasn't difficult and I didn't mind so much. I enjoyed living in different apartments and exploring different *barrios*. I'd never lived in an apartment before moving to Buenos Aires—so I was getting my fill of it in mid-life. I found the perfect place in Recoleta through the newcomers' community. It was two blocks away from my therapist and a short bus ride to Estudio DNI. The owner lived in London and would be back for a month over Christmas but I could stay until then and return after the New Year.

The elevator only went to the eighteenth floor and I had to lug my cases up the extra floor. There were only two apartments on the nineteenth floor and I was right across from the door to the roof, so I could easily get outside in the mornings before it got too hot. From my kitchen window I could see Uruguay: A sliver between an azure sky and the murky sienna Rio de la Plata. Ocean vessels floated by and on weekends sailboats glided across the surface of the river. Planes drew diagonals across the sky—ascending and descending. The view was a welcome upgrade from windows overlooking little more than cement.

Various shades of green sent much-needed oxygen up to the nineteenth floor and I could breathe again. My lungs had a chance to eliminate the secondhand smoke and exhaust fumes that enveloped me when I lived close to the street where vehicles and pedestrians scurried about in circles. My cough subsided.

Up above the world, in all this modern, luminous space, I relaxed, expanded, and embraced a new perspective. I could see farther. From up there, I could see the future and its limitless possibility.

Ж

Trevor was a writer for the Buenos Aires Herald, an English newspaper that was published every Sunday. I was seduced by his words.

From: tangueraontour
To: trevor@buenosairesherald.com
Subject: Who are you?

Dear Trevor,

I just read your most recent piece in the Herald. I wish more men had your insight and courage regarding women. I loved it. I'm curious about you.

I'm writer and artist with a strong interest in gender studies. My initial plan upon arriving in Buenos Aires was to write a book about Tango as a metaphor for communication between the masculine and feminine.

I'd like to invite you to our writers group. We meet every Wednesday morning on Corrientes near Montevideo. It would be great to meet you and have a discussion about the man/women relationship.

Maraya

From: Trevor
To: Maraya
Subject: Re: Who are you?

Dear Maraya,

Thank you for the lovely message. Living in Buenos Aires for over 15 years has been transformative. Writing, like performing on stage, is an edgy experience. You are always either leaning over that edge or shying away from it. Over and over, experience confirms that it is better to lean over the edge. I leaned over in last week's column ... and look what I got in return.

It would be nice to sit and talk with you in a B.A. cafe.

Trevor

From: Maraya
To: Trevor
Subject: Re: Who are you?

Hi Trevor,

I've just relocated to Recoleta and will be attending the 4-day Robert McKee STORY workshop starting Thursday. I hope it propels my writing into the next dimension. I don't seem to be able to maintain my edge.

What brought and held you here for so many years? Do you tango? What else? These and many other questions are best answered over coffee. I'm looking forward to meeting you.

Maraya

Ж

The weekend after I moved, I took Robert McKee's STORY seminar. McKee is not only a master of the written word, he is a kick-ass guru. If you understand story structure and character development as well as he does, you understand life and human nature. The workshop was the best therapy I'd had in a long time and it gave me the courage to take a realistic look at my relationship with Jesse. We'd had three weekends in a row of fighting and no loving. Despite all our deep conversations, our relationship had deteriorated dramatically. I was tired, frustrated and disappointed. There was no future for us, there never had been. I'd moved farther away from him…and higher up; I felt I'd made a massive change from the gutter to the clouds. I had to end it.

So, a week later, after another argument, I knew before I got to his place how it would turn out. I'd put my jacket on and was standing in the entryway. He went into another room saying, "I need to take a shower and a nap."

"Goodbye, Jesse."

From the other side of the closed door I heard him, surprised, "You're leaving?"

Yes. This time I closed the door.

From: Jesse
To: Maraya

Subject: Can't we just Tango?

Why does it have to be this way? Why can't we still dance? Why does it have to be all or nothing? Why must you want more than what you have? I would love to dance with you still ... I will miss you at the *milonga*. We can back off of other "fronts," but why do we need to back off from all? The "issues" we have are solely within the domain of a "couple" not a couple of dancers.

/j

From: Maraya
To: Jesse
Subject: Re: Can't we just Tango?

NO. Maybe you believe you could just tango. But, when two people have shared and cared deeply for each other as we have, I think it's naïve to believe we can return to a time before tango became more than just a dance. I'm not built that way. There is no forgetting, there is no regressing—no going back. Case in point—you have not been able to let go and heal your past relationships and that has gotten in the way of this one and that's one reason why we are here where we are now. Once we have tasted the bliss of a deep connection, no matter what fear guards those places, there is that pleasure-seeking part of ourselves, that place that yearns for love and intimacy, that will always want to taste it again.

To arrange to dance we would have to communicate. To work out a pattern, to take a class, we would have to negotiate how to do it. To go to a *milonga* we would have to socialize, drink, spend time together. We would end up sharing a meal and engaging in deep conversation, like we used to. A good night kiss on the cheek would not be enough. We could never go back to the cheek. I want sex. Some of the best memories were those sublime Sunday mornings when we would wake up and share our dreams and make love, then rise late and explore a new place for brunch. Engaging in a stirring conversation—you witnessing my life, me witnessing yours—this is far more than just dancing tango. We can't ignore nor deny those

192

countless moments we shared that were the tango of life and of relationship and not just a dance.

No, my dear, we cannot *just* tango.

Take care,

Maraya

CHAPTER 35
A Poetic Tryst

I suppose we're all fictions in other people's lives.

Kevin Carrel Footer

From: Maraya
To: Trevor
Subject: What happened to our wordplay?

Hi Trevor,

I thought we'd made a nice connection with our words and that the wordplay would continue for a bit—and maybe we'd meet. I'm disappointed that you haven't replied.

Maraya

From: Trevor
To: Maraya
Subject: Re: What happened to our wordplay?

Dearest Maraya,

Please forgive my silence. I treasure your words and have been thinking of you. My life has been a whirlwind with rehearsals, radio and TV shows with the band. Believe me, you have been on my mind—but my life hasn't been mine.

That said, and with last night's show behind me, I would love to meet you. When would be a good time for you?

I have an idea. You said you've been photographing the Recoleta Cemetery. Let's meet there. You pick the tomb.

I'm looking forward very much to meeting.

Trevor

From: Maraya
To: Trevor
Subject: Re: What happened to our wordplay?

Dear Trevor,

I'd love to meet you. Sunday? I don't know the tombs by number. Let's meet in the central area where the benches are. What's a good time for you? (Not early please).

Maraya,

From: Trevor
To: Maraya
Subject: Re: What happened to our wordplay?

Spoken like a good *tanguero*. not too early. Let's meet Sunday at 2 p.m. I'll be wearing a black hat and I will stroll down that central alley until you reveal yourself to me.

Trevor

Resuscitation

Autumn's sun painted heavy shadows behind us and already I was too warm. We sought sanctuary, walking among the aisles of the aggrandized in eternal homes, more intent on exploring the inner passages of each other than those of the necropolis. In the shade we sat, upon the steps of the tomb of the family Prat.

"You know nothing about me," I said.

"I know a lot about you."

"How so? Did you google me?"

"No."

"Then you know nothing about me."

"I know you from your words."

"From your first message, I felt as if you were courting me."

"I am."

He pierced me with his gaze as if he might part the veils and strip me of defenses: my nervous laughter and rapid-fire questions to keep him talking. Perhaps the cousins of the words that brought us together could explain why, and predict our future. But the air filled with incomplete thoughts, half-formed sentences, jagged phrasing softened by tender possibility. No safety in answers.

We are all travellers, walking among the dead, seeking companionship, collaboration for a profound inner journey, however brief. We are all searching for something to keep us from becoming ashes to dust from the inside out before our time.

"Who are you?"

"I am the man who wants to be with you."

He lay his back down on the cool marble, head at my feet, and shifted his gaze toward the sky between the sepulchral sculptures. I suppressed the desire to lean over and place my mouth upon his.

From: Trevor
To: Maraya
Subject: The muse and the music

Maraya (a name I already love),

So nice to meet you. What you wrote is so fucking beautiful.

Trevor

From: Maraya
To: Trevor
Subject: Re: The muse and the music

Querida Poeta,

Muchisima gracias. I'm enjoying playing with the story, with the possibility of what comes next, imagining the dialogue, the filming of a tango in the cemetery, and the music that turns it into a moving visual art piece. I want to make a movie. Let's make a movie.

That phone number will often reach me, but it somehow seems right for two writers to write. Poetry preferred in print. There are other conversations to have face to face—and dancing to be done. I am game—you are the hunter. Let's dance.

Maraya

From: Trevor
To: Maraya
Subject: Re: The muse and the music

Maraya,

[sound of a careening car and screeching brakes ... then the scent of a mysterious perfume wafting across the set] Yes, let's make a movie. I'm looking forward to writing the script.

197

Today I am consecrated to music and will let my prey escape my claws. For now. I perform tonight and will spend the rest of the day on my journey toward that moment. Perhaps we can dance together at some afternoon milonga.

One soft kiss placed on the part of your body you most fear revealing to my inquisitioning eyes. (You choose.)

Trevor

[sound of a herd of horses galloping across the plains]

From: Maraya
To: Trevor
Subject: Re: The muse and the music

In the anti-classic/anti-structure/Art film style, I hear fewer cars crashing and fewer horses hooves (except for the clopping on cobblestones) and more moans, cries and whispers; I see ephemeral images dancing between tombs, sunlight glinting off polished marble, shadows shifting uncomfortably, and looming sculptures— the only witnesses.

I will leave my phone on.

M

From: Trevor
To: Maraya
Subject: Re: The muse and the music

Beautiful Maraya,

I want to play. Let's dance Friday afternoon.

Trevor

From: Maraya
To: Trevor
Subject: Re: The muse and the music

You are a mystery, more like a ghost to me. Confitería Ideal, Friday at 2:00.

Maraya

Ж

One Afternoon at Confitería Ideal

The nature of tango forces us to protect ourselves in subtle ways from the inherent vulnerability it presents. We press ourselves against a stranger's body and move as one. We can feel under the skin of the other; we can smell them; our perspiration mingles—on our hands, our brows, our backs. In any other situation this might be too close for comfort. How does it become "comfortable" on the dance floor? We adopt an internal protective attitude. We close our eyes. We try to surrender.

Enough words had been exchanged; it was time to feel. We made a silent pact to be unprotected in our humanness with each other. Virtual strangers, we had chosen to dance a delicious forbidden tango.

Where else but Buenos Aires can you dance tango in the middle of the day? It is called Ideal: the ideal confitería for a lovers' tryst. A venerable restaurant and dance hall built in 1912, the walls are lined with dark wooden panels; large columns hold up a ceiling with a stained-glass domed skylight; huge mirrors reflect patrons and formally attired, properly nonchalant, waiters.

I arrive first, wearing a vintage linen dress in a style of the 1940s. Its pale golden colour is highlighted by an ivory trim on the fitted v-neck empire-waist bodice; it has an A-line skirt to allow legs freedom for dancing. Had I accessorized with a vintage hat and gloves, the "Golden Era" fantasy would be complete. I choose a table, change my shoes, and order a drink. I dreamily watch the couples glide across the dance floor.

199

Minutes later, he strides in and over to a table on the other side of the room. He doesn't want to sit with me; he wants to play. I feign disinterest, pretend not to look, pretend to not want to dance with him. I can't fake it. He is too beautiful and he wants me. I'm drawn to his eyes like a magnet and we coquettishly go through the ritual: eye contact, nod, rise, meet on la pista.

He invites me into his embrace. I surrender. For a moment, we stand together, close, motionless, breathing in each other's scent. I feel him move and I obey. I only want to go where he wants me to go. His embrace assures me that I am safe—at least for this song, for this moment—and this moment is all we have, all that matters.

He turns me for an ocho and his hand edges close to where the flesh leaves my ribs and rises. My breath catches, becomes shallow and quickens. My breasts are pressed against his chest. I hope the sound of my heart isn't too loud. My temple against his—I hope my thoughts don't distract him. He is so close, so close I can feel his past, present and future. I can smell his desire. My thigh brushes up against the front of his trousers. His breath is on my neck, in my ear, surrounding my disconnected thoughts.

Between songs, we separate, maintaining a publicly approved intimate distance, and gaze into each other's eyes—searching for understanding.

"You look stunning," he whispers. I blush.

During the cortinas, we sit together, no longer willing to waste precious little time playing games across the floor. Still, we speak very little.

"What kind of agreement do you have with your wife regarding other women?"

"It's very Argentine."

"But you're not. What does that mean?"

"She understands my need to dance."

He tries to maintain machismo but I can tell he's uncomfortable with my line of inquiry. I stop. We dance a couple more tandas and, too soon, it is time for him to slip away.

I bend down to change my shoes and hide the tears welling up in my eyes. This is the last I will see of him. So much has been left undone.

200

CHAPTER 36

Going to God

It was more than 25 years since I'd first heard about João de Deus. Early in my search for enlightenment, I had been a voracious reader of other people's journeys. One of the first books I'd read was Shirley MacLaine's *Dancing in the Light*; she relays an account of her visit to Abadiania, Brazil to visit the spiritual healer and medium known as John of God. I was intrigued but hadn't thought much more about it at the time; Brazil was too far off my radar as a travel destination. John's name likely passed through my experience again as I investigated many different New Age modalities and gurus. But, if so, I hadn't paid attention. I had nothing to heal.

Several years ago, my parents took a trip to Brazil with friends who were regulars at the Casa de Dom Inácio de Loyola in Abadiania—the healing centre of John of God. They didn't have any major health problems—just minor manifestations of the chronic conditions that typically accompany older age: arthritis, and elevated cholesterol, blood sugar, and blood pressure levels.

My mother had been told by her doctor that she would require major abdominal surgery to correct a minor chronic problem that was not debilitating but only mildly annoying. She chose to live with it rather than risk surgery. But the problem was at the top of her list of issues to be healed by John. And, it was healed; the problem disappeared. An even bigger mystery revealed itself upon her return home: when she relayed her experience to a friend, the friend admitted she had had the same problem and, while my mother was away, her friend experienced the same healing at home. Meanwhile, during the visit, my stepfather's hernia disappeared. While at the Casa, they witnessed "surgeries" performed on others and heard of several miraculous healings.

One of the main reasons my friend Phil was even in Buenos Aires was because of its proximity to Abadiania. He'd felt drawn to visit the Casa and other spiritual centres in the area. About a year ago, after he'd returned to B.A. from his first visit to Abadiania, we met at Astro's, a small cafe across the street from Vero's apartment. Phil pulled out his laptop and began to show me his photos one by one, telling a story for each.

After two hours of hearing about various miracles and seeing photo upon photo of orbs (still not totally convinced they're other than artifacts of flash photography), I became restless and had to stifle my yawns. Phil turned off the computer.

"Put your hands out like this," he motioned, then reached into his back pocket. "I have something for you."

I complied, cupping my hands in front of me. He was acting mysterious and I became curious.

"One day, when I was leaving the Casa," he began, "I saw John get into a taxi. He sat there for a moment. I couldn't see what he was doing, but then he popped something into his mouth and tossed something out the window. After he drove away, I went over to see what it was. I don't normally pick up other people's trash, but I was drawn to retrieve this." Phil placed the cellophane candy wrapper into my outstretched hands.

I was instantly filled with emotion. I burst into tears and sobbed uncontrollably for several minutes, glad to be facing the wall, while Phil tenderly sat with me. I couldn't explain what had happened, nor could I sufficiently describe the feeling that came over me as I held the little piece of trash. It felt like being filled with love.

At that time, it was early in my sabbatical and I was still filled with hope and expectation. I had no reason to see a spiritual healer. I was convinced I could fix my own problems. But, a year later, I was nearing the end of my sabbatical and felt I hadn't quite worked out how to support myself upon my return to Canada; I didn't feel the least bit enlightened. It wasn't until I had given up in frustration, desperate for answers, that I sought spiritual intervention. Although not exactly sure what I needed, upon meeting Phil for coffee after his third visit to the Casa, I intuited that it was finally time for me to go, to surrender to the possibility that I, like so many other seekers, might receive help from the "other world" through the medium, John of God.

I secured a Brazilian visa and shopped for the appropriate white attire as requested by the Casa guidelines. Apparently it's easier to see one's aura when one wears white. I was proud to have packed two weeks' worth of whites and other casual clothes in one carry-on suitcase. But when I got to the airport, early morning a week later, I had to check my bag because it was three kilos overweight. *Make the fat guy with his backpack, his briefcase and his duty-free bag pay extra!* Skinny me would have to wait for my one small bag, carefully chosen and delicately packed, at the carousel after arrival.

My boarding pass stated a boarding time fifteen minutes later than my departure time. The monitor showed a departure time as "estimated." *Odd.* Other passengers with boarding passes for the same flight showed a boarding time 45 minutes prior to departure. It soon became apparent, as we all congregated at the gate, that there was a problem. That's what happens when countries can't get their acts together around daylight savings time. It was now past the updated departure time, nearing the original departure time, and we were told we would be given an update soon…by noon. After that, things went smoothly.

We arrived in Brasilia in the dark. A taxi driver had been sent to fetch me and an elderly couple from South Africa, and he drove us for an hour to our mutual lodgings in Abadiania. I liked Donna and David immediately. They sat close together in the back seat, shining like beacons of love, light and spirituality, with their clear blue eyes and white hair. Our first task was to find a cooperative bank machine in order to withdraw enough *reaies* for the duration since we would be somewhat isolated and restricted for two weeks. No such luck.

It was dark at the Pousada Caminho Encantado when we arrived—as if Walter, the owner, wasn't expecting us. My room, at the end of the garden, wasn't ready: the floor was unswept, there was no soap and almost no toilet paper. *Was I supposed to bring my own or pay extra for those essentials?* My bed appeared clean and I was too tired to care. After indulging in some of the blessed water that Phil had thoughtfully left for me, I crawled between the sheets and was soon dreaming of crumbling structures.

DAY 1

Morning revealed a verdant landscape outside my substantial window: rolling hills with patches of forest and an azure sky bursting with clouds. My room was large, recently constructed, modestly furnished and decorated mostly in white. It had a pleasant zen-like quality, nothing disruptive to the eye. It was snuggled in a row of six such rooms, motel style, with a short distance through the garden to the main house where we gathered for meals.

I enjoyed a buffet-style breakfast on the patio with the other residents of the *pousada,* all there to visit John. We got to know each other briefly before walking the short kilometre across the red dust lanes to the Casa for the orientation.

204

João Teixeira de Faria was born in 1942. He grew up poor with only two years of formal education. He became aware, as a young boy, that he had the gift of mediumship. In 1978, John began to fulfill his life's purpose by performing healing work in the small Brazilian village of Abadiania. Initially, he just sat on a chair near the main road and people soon began to arrive, seeking cures for various illnesses and conditions. Gradually, more and more people sought his help and, eventually, João established the Casa de Dom Inácio de Loyola.

The Casa compound consisted of several one-story buildings and was situated at the eastern edge of town. All structures were painted white, trimmed in blue, and surrounded by manicured lawns and lush green gardens bursting with flowers. Wooden benches were thoughtfully placed for rest and contemplation. Hundreds of people, from all over the world, congregated in the main hall and spilled out of the open-air pavilion onto the steps and into the gardens. Almost everyone was dressed in white, with the odd rebel, pauper, or uninformed, in modest dark attire. Everyone seemed eager and hopeful, wanting to hear the instructions for the day, waiting to find out their place in the line that would file past John.

There was a low stage on the far end of the outdoor meeting area and a small wooden triangle hung on the back wall behind it. People approached the wall to pray and stuff photos and slips of paper into the frame with hope of receiving healing for family members and friends back home.

Diego, one of the volunteers, approached the microphone and proceeded to explain the protocol in English to those of us who had just arrived. After him, another man began to speak, and continued to go on and on in Portuguese. I had no idea what he was talking about but it didn't sound soft or spiritual; his voice had a sharp edge to it. Maybe that was the way he expressed his passion, but I didn't like it. Although the Casa is a non-denominational spiritual "hospital," not a church, there was a decidedly Christian vibe to it. We were, after all, in a predominantly Catholic country. He sounded like he was preaching.

We were all told to write down our request—one or two words—but I still didn't know what to ask for. John channelled spirits of deceased physicians and other masters of healing. I sort of trusted that the Entities, in their capable omniscience, knew better than I did about what I needed.

Requests were presented to John by one of his volunteers as we each approached him in a fairly quick-moving queue. But, prior to that, I sat on the ass-pressing pew in the anteroom with a crowd of others, listening to canned music on repeat, eyes closed, arms and legs uncrossed so as not to impede the flow of energy. I've never been one for praying, and I sucked at meditation, but I sat obligingly and waited for something to happen. And waited ...

We took a break for lunch and sat at outdoor tables with our bowls of homemade soup. After lunch, I had a crystal bed session. I lay on my back on what was much like a massage bed. Above each of my seven chakras hung a crystal with a coloured light that corresponded to that particular chakra, and emitted healing energy through it. The time spent in repose was somewhat relaxing, but not otherwise enlightening nor healing—that I noticed.

I sat, again, in the anteroom for the afternoon session. After an hour, my positive spiritual facade began to show signs of wear. The Portuguese proselytizer's voice carried into our room from outside and he droned on and on for another two hours. But, we were supposed to focus on ourselves and stay connected. *Connected to what? I'm lousy at thinking about nothing.* I didn't feel connected or inspired or spiritual or much of anything except ensuing annoyance and a sore butt.

By the end of the day, it was our turn—those of us waiting less than patiently in the annex—to parade before John and receive our instructions. Although I had seen pictures, they compared not at all to passing before John of God in the flesh.

He was a foreboding figure: over six feet tall with thinning dark hair and soft brown eyes—that looked vacant when he was in a trance-like state. In that moment he was not himself, but an empty vessel being used for the greater good. I received a "prescription" to visit the waterfall. No surgery for me...yet. I was glad to escape church for the day and head down the road to discover something new and a little more fun.

Fruitties was the hub on the corner at the intersection of the main dirt thoroughfare at the east end of the village. Owned by an understanding and enterprising expat, the cafe served good coffee, smoothies, wraps and healthy baked goods. They offered a vegetarian buffet every Friday. It was a popular place to congregate.

I found a comfy couch upstairs where I could look out onto the main intersection. Phil cycled over and we spent the afternoon chatting. It was good to have a knowledgeable friend to share my observations and experiences with. He introduced me to Billy and Allie, a young couple from New Zealand, and I liked them right away. They didn't seem to have any ailments; they were just in town for the adventure. Billy had brought his guitar, he composed his own songs. We discussed the possibility of organizing an evening of music and poetry—sort of an open mic—on the coming weekend. I soon said good-bye to my new friends and headed down the road to the *pousada* for dinner.

DAY 2

I'd dreamed that a guy was droning on and on like a newscaster. Then, a new guy came on the scene after him and went on and on the same way. I noticed a tiny microphone lapel pin that clearly said: spleen revision. It made no sense to me until I googled it in the morning. Chinese medicine believes spleen energy gets depleted in travellers and needs to be replenished so that all other systems are nourished. That made complete sense to me. I was subtly suffering the consequences of being uprooted. I needed more stability, more routine, more home and more tender touch. Finally something concrete: I needed to heal my spleen.

During the second day of sitting and "praying" and other Casa activities, my spiritual intervention was booked for the following day: Friday the thirteenth. I prepared by watching Phil's pre-release copy of a film about John and the Casa. Maybe it was not such a good idea as it showed graphic "surgeries." But, I was told the visual surgeries were not as commonly performed anymore unless someone specifically requested one in order to believe what they could not simply have faith in.

DAY 3

I was nervous, probably because of what I'd seen in the movie and partly because they referred to it as "surgery" which holds unfavourable connotations that "spiritual intervention" does not —at least for me. After sitting for a time, a group of us passed by John and into the annex—the surgery room—where we sat while John's spiritual associates, the Entities, worked us over. I didn't feel a thing. After a short time of more sitting, we filed out and I went to the dispensary to receive my herbs: *pasiflor* (passion flower) blessed by the Entities and infused with each individual's unique prescription. They all came out of the same drawer.

I didn't take a taxi back to my *pousada* as instructed. My bad. I felt well enough to walk so I did. I was required to stay in my room, to stay in bed actually, and sleep for twenty-four hours. I wasn't that tired. How long would I have to take those herbs and avoid spicy foods, wine and sex? Sixty days? Well,…no sex wouldn't be a problem…and finding spicy food in Argentina was like finding blossoms in the desert, but no Malbec? What would I drink with my steak?

A staff member brought dinner to my room and I entertained myself by watching the clouds change and float by my window while birds flirted in the trees. Dusk settled and I slept and dreamed of tango.

DAY 4

Breakfast was brought to me. There was no WiFi in my room so I watched the forested grassy hills meet an ever-changing sky and put pen to paper hoping an astonishing array of words would appear. Twice around the clock I had whiled away in my room, feeling like a youngster who had been grounded. By late afternoon I was allowed to go out again and play…but there was not much to do. I checked my email, found a copy of Shirley McLaine's *Dancing in the Light* in the common area and started rereading it. I had to stay out of the direct sunlight and I wasn't allowed to exercise for a week until after my internal stitches were magically removed in the middle of the night. *Sheesh!* I wasn't sick and I didn't actually have surgery—not "real" surgery. I felt antsy.

DAY 5

From: Maraya
To: Bill
Subject: Going to God

Hi Bill,

I'm in the middle of Nowhere, Brazil, in a small community that reminds me of all the small towns we stayed in on our trip to Mexico (but the doors are less interesting). Abadiania is everything Buenos Aires is not. Or, better said, Buenos Aires is everything and Abadiania is not. This makes it a welcome reprieve from the big city. You would love it here. I skipped church this morning because I can only take so much Christianity and I am surprised at how well I am taking it—surrendering to it and letting whatever spiritual work be done on me that needs to be.

This is a magical place. I have met more clear, blue-eyed foreigners (like you!) than I could have imagined—kindred spirits. My "people" are travellers in search of healing and enlightenment. They have come from everywhere: Capetown, Dublin, New Zealand. Every day I enjoy a fruit smoothie high in antioxidants and lovingly prepared at the cafe where we congregate when we are not in session three days a week. Every day I feel immense love and gentleness and curiosity and healing energy around me. I never thought I'd find myself here—and what a surprise—here I am … and still hoping to find myself….

This will be one of the few places in the world that I'll find difficult to leave. I will want to return to this feeling of community, peace and fullness (peacefulness).

I hope you're well.

Maraya

CHAPTER 37

Miracles Happen ... But Not For Me

For those who believe—no proof is necessary.
For those who disbelieve—no amount of proof is sufficient.

Stuart Chase

DAY 6

The Casa would not be in session again until Wednesday and there wasn't much to do but read and write and heal and rest and mosey down to the corner to talk to others at the meeting and eating places. International friendships were made easily in this place where all superficiality falls away. It was easy to sit and chat for hours, listen to all the interesting stories: chronic fatigue brought on by surgery after an accident; a lost arm after an infected mosquito bite followed by lowered immunity; a full-body cancer condensed into the tip of a little finger; constant brain seizures subsiding only while within close proximity to the energetic enter of the Casa de Dom Inácio. For some, the visit is a desperate attempt, a last resort, and they come armed with faith in miracles. And miracles do happen. For others, it's too late or it's a step toward the next possibility.

Billy and I planned a "sharing of talents" event for the following night, before sessions began again. He and Allie were supposed to head home but Allie slipped and hurt her back—she hadn't wanted to leave so she created a good excuse not to. It was unfortunate that she had to hurt herself to get what she wanted; the rest of us were glad they stayed.

Alone in my room for too long, my temporarily-suppressed skeptic started grumbling a request for acknowledgement. So, I headed to the main house to appease it by searching the internet for articles about John. I hadn't come to the Casa because I either believed or disbelieved. I figured as long as I maintained an attitude of "not knowing" I could remain curious and leave myself open to experience miracles and learning. Once I closed my mind and accepted a rigid certainty, I would no longer be a student.

The western analytical mind attempts to debunk what it doesn't understand, is afraid of, or can't control. How do you explain unsterilized incisions not causing infections, and inner stitches found by ultrasound with no accompanying outer incision, and the improved health, if not full curing, of so many?

If you see something, or experience it with your other senses, does that make it real? According to some naysayers, the eye-scraping surgery and the forceps up the nose are carnival tricks. Maybe so. But, they can't explain all the miracles that take place away from the watchful eye. We have enough science to support the fact that there is more to this world than meets the eye—and the other senses. Just because we don't understand something doesn't mean it's not "real."

Allopathic medicine has its place in dealing with emergencies but it's often lousy at treating chronic and terminal conditions. And, even if a person seeks alternative treatment, that doesn't mean there will be relief there either. Sometimes "healing" provides only peaceful assistance to the next experience. None of us knows our future.

John charges nothing to anyone who wishes to visit him for healing. It costs nothing to sit in the current of the Entities. It costs nothing to receive spiritual intervention. It costs nothing to receive a bowl of blessed nutritious soup each of the three days per week that the Casa is open. The Casa is operated by volunteers and funded by donations. It does, however, cost ten *reais* for a bottle of herbs. They may be effective and maybe not. But, if not, the placebo effect—the belief in relief—is powerful enough in itself to cause change. It costs twenty *reais* for a 20-minute crystal-bed treatment—which may do something ... and may not. But, it's not detrimental and it's definitely relaxing. It costs the same for blessed water as any other kind of bottled water.

The price of accommodations and food in restaurants was reasonable, not overblown as in so many other tourist areas. There was no indication anyone was getting rich (except in spirit) doing the work. I got no sense of cultism or price gouging at the Casa or in the village. The whole area felt welcoming, loving and healing. So, then, what would be the incentive, the reason, for performing carnival tricks and promoting healing if healing was not really occurring?

I found no evidence of a scam. I'd made a solid attempt to satisfy my skeptic but I found the attempt at debunking by others to be flimsy—flimsier than the many positive effects I had heard about—even if I hadn't experienced a miracle for myself.

DAY 7

I woke up at 5:00 a.m. in order to go to the waterfall before dawn. I'd missed out a few days earlier when I hadn't wanted to rise so early. Getting up in the dark to stand under a cold spray was not appealing, but it was part of the process I'd committed to so I forced myself. Five of us drove to the Casa then down the hill to a forested area. Dawn was peeking as we parked.

David and Billy went down the path first; we were not allowed to go in mixed company. We also weren't allowed to stay more than a few minutes so they were back in no time and it was the girls' turn. Donna, Allie and I took the short path, single file, through the trees to the small waterfall and pool. We each took a turn at the falls alone, and stood there for a reverent moment while the other two respectfully held back.

I'd seen my share of waterfalls. This one, although not spectacular, moved me to tears as I stood before it in the half-light of dawn. I hadn't intended to go under but I dipped my foot in the spray—not as cold as falls fed by the Rockies. It would have been nice to spend more time alone in that natural setting but there was a limit imposed on communing with the gods so we returned to the car and back to our *pousada* for breakfast.

In the evening, a large group of us enjoyed the vegetarian buffet at Fruitties and some of us shared our spoken word and music with the group. Food, friends, and music—my favourite kind of evening; I enjoyed myself immensely.

DAY 8

It was Wednesday again, and the first day of round two at the spiritual hospital. I had dreamed that Gerry wanted to get back together. He'd told me in a previous dream that he wouldn't be back anymore. But, this was the anniversary of our separation nineteen years earlier. Coincidentally, it also marked the day of my father's death. November had always been a difficult month for me. Maybe my ex just wanted to check in and give me his blessing. *Ha!* I chose to "celebrate" the inauspicious day in church seeking absolution … or some other kind of solution.

I was tired and my body hurt. I didn't look forward to sitting in the current. Actually, the current would be fine; it was the wooden pew I didn't look forward to. Probably as little as a year ago, or two, I wouldn't have been able to be in this place. The

214

deep Christian base would have rankled me and I would have had my defenses up. Still, I couldn't fully embrace it even now. I'd been resistant to opening my mouth to recite the Lord's Prayer—although I followed it in my head as trained in childhood. I'd been resistant to organized religion most of my life. It had played a part in the dissolution of both my marriages. It was probably a good thing that most of what was said was in Portuguese since I couldn't react to what I didn't understand.

While in the translation line, Diego suggested I ask to sit in the current room. Once John granted that, he could work on my other requests there. *One step closer to God...* "Excellent," I said. "That's what I'd prefer." I didn't want surgery again because I didn't want to buy and take more herbs and extend my abstinence by two more months. That would be inconvenient.

It felt like my last chance to ask for something tangible—help with what I wanted and wasn't able to manifest on my own. I asked for the removal of whatever was in the way of me attracting my soulmate. The interpreter just wrote "soulmate" on a little piece of paper. I also asked for help with my writing. My list wasn't even read.

"Surgery today at two o'clock."

Damn. Apparently my healing schedule was out of my hands and not meant to be convenient.

If you're generally a believer, or at least open-minded, at what point do you finally hit the wall of your faith? For me it was this: When I arrived at the surgery room, after sitting in the current and then parading before John, there was standing room only. I had already felt the energy and now I was weak. I expected something big—a major shift—or at least the chance to meditate in the surgery room and honour my traumatic anniversary day. I tried to get comfortable standing for what might be a while when a booming voice in Portuguese said, "In the name of the Father," signalling the end before anything had begun for those of us who had entered the room at the end of the line. We, the standing, were told to file out first. I thought we were getting kicked out—to return another time. But, no, we were done; the session was over. I felt ripped off. That had been my last chance for intervention.

How long should surgery last? How long does it take the Entities to perform an intervention? Would I have been satisfied with ten minutes? An hour? How long would have been too long? And, during that time, what did I expect to feel? What should have happened for me to be satisfied? Well,... SOMETHING!

We were told to take a taxi home and sleep—but not before we stood in line to get another six bottles of innocuous herbs infused with our own special energetic prescription. We had all received the same piece of paper, saying as much, prior to surgery, and we all got six bottles out of the same drawer dumped into a plastic bag and were charged 60 *reais*.

I had planned to take a taxi but my skepticism-infused rebelliousness took over and I walked. *If you don't follow the rules of the game you chose to play then how can you expect to win?* Walking did little to burn off steam. My irritation was piquing. I told Walter I didn't want any dinner and that the door next to my room squeaked like crazy and needed oil.

I didn't feel sick; I wasn't tired. I was "banished" again to my room and I honestly was hungry but I didn't want to eat. Even so, the cook arrived at my door with my meal and could see I was irritated by the comings and goings of my noisy neighbour. That's not all I was irritated with but she couldn't fix the rest. She returned shortly with a bottle of olive oil and poured some on the hinges of my neighbour's door. That made me smile.

DAY 9

Last night I had my stitches out from my previous week's spiritual spleen surgery while I slept. I dreamed about Gerry again. We were going to get back together. He'd lost weight, and looked like he had when we'd married; he wore a wine-coloured blazer with lapels textured like my grandparents' old sofa. That antique piece of furniture had graced our living room. We were sitting close and I felt such love; I thought that even if he hadn't changed during all those years, I had. So, maybe I could make our marriage work this time.

I wished I'd slept longer. I didn't want to stay in my room. I got up in time to get some fruit from the breakfast table, then checked my email and my bank account online. That certainly didn't make me feel any better. I felt depressed, scared, negative and skeptical. *Best to sleep it off.* I went back to my room for the remainder of the day.

DAY 10

It was my last day at the Casa. I had asked to sit in the main current room but they neglected to grant permission the day before since they had been in such a hurry to usher me out of surgery. With a little encouragement from Billy, I decided to sit there anyway. The morning wasn't too bad, but by afternoon I was tired of hearing Eidelweiss for the fourth time; I'm not sure what that song has to do with healing in Brazil; it only made me think of *The Sound of Music*. No matter how I sat, my spine was on hardwood and I couldn't meditate nor feel energy nor contribute to the group. I was bored and uncomfortable.

When Billy started rustling beside me, I opened my eyes to see that it was time to go up for the goodbye line. As we approached, they were preparing to do a visible operation—the only one since we'd arrived. It was to be an eye scraping. The photographers blocked my view, but it didn't matter; I'd seen it on video. Afterward, the patient was wheeled past us in a chair, eyes closed, serene expression on her face.

When I went up to express my gratitude for whatever had happened to me during my stay, John was poised to write and just stopped, stared, and said nothing. That was it.

DAY 11

Miracles had happened all around but none had happened for me; none that I was aware of. But then, I hadn't asked for anything immediately tangible. The work of the Entities was to continue long after we left, but we would have to do our part. I didn't know exactly what that would be.

I said goodbye to Phil. Allie, Billy and I shared a cab to the airport. Allie was sick. She kept creating illnesses because she didn't want to leave the magic. There was a horrendous line at the airport check-in so, while they decided to go sightseeing before boarding their flight, I elected to skip out on visiting the famous blue glass cathedral of Brasilia and stand in line.

While I waited for my connecting flight in Sao Paulo, I recognized a couple from the Casa and we ended up sharing a taxi into central Buenos Aires after the second leg of our journey. They got dropped off first. The *taxista* mistook me for a tourist and tried to cheat me out of 100 pesos. But, since I'd lived in the city long enough to have heard several stories of taxi scammery, I foiled his attempt and departed with an indignant huff.

In the middle of the night, Billy phoned. He and Allie were stranded—no hostel and no luggage—so they came over and took the bed while I slept on the couch. In the morning they took off to explore the city and find a hostel for a couple days before they returned to New Zealand.

From: Maraya
To: Phil
Subject: Post holiday blues

Hi Phil,

I need someone to talk to. Please indulge me. It'll be like me journalling and thinking there's someone on the other end listening.

I went to John almost as a last resort: full of hope, and maybe some desperation. I don't know exactly what I expected to get out of it—miracles maybe. I expected to continue feeling as well when I got back to B.A. as I had in Abadiania. Is this why people keep going back? To keep soaking up those soft feelings of peace, love and hope?

I feel like I got nothing out of it. I mean, nothing from John or the Entities. Whatever I "got" was from the humans I met there. I met some fabulous people and felt a lot of love. I didn't have any otherworldly experiences. Felt nothing but lots of energy at times—which could just have been from a gathering of enlightened humans. I don't know … I'll continue to take the herbs and maintain faith of some sort. It's difficult to not drink Malbec—especially with *bife de lomo*, pasta, or when I feel down.

I felt so creative, inspired and motivated in Abadiania. I couldn't stop thinking about my projects. That's all dissipated. My travel debt is accumulating and my way out of it is not. I don't even feel excited about the time I have left in B.A. I do want to find a way to make the most of it before I return to Canada.

Sooo … what am I supposed to do about it? Just stop, forget about it? Wait? Relax?

Post spiritual holiday blues. I'll cut and colour my hair, go dancing and prepare for next week's trip—south to the mountains of Patagonia and then to the Land of Fire—Ushuaia. I am excited about that. I'll get busy and distracted and move on.

219

Thanks for reading me. I miss your shiny, smiley face. I didn't even get pictures of orbs. Please send me a couple of your favourites and please say a prayer for me while you're still there to help speed up my process.

Abrazo grande,

Maraya

From: Phil
To: Maraya
Subject: Re: Post holiday blues

Hi Maraya,

Lo siento mi amiga. Que duro. I think you intuited the answer when you summed up: "So, what am I supposed to do about it?"

Nothing. Or, by nothing I mean you could practice nothingness kinds of things like meditation, prayer, yoga, Qi Gong, or whatever you know to practice (tango?) that shifts your energy in a good direction.

"Just stop, forget about it?" *Si.*
"Wait?" *Si, si.*
"Relax?" *Si, si, si, claro que si.*

Relax is the word to which the entire Course in Miracles distills itself and it can't be overstated. Now, that's all easy to say. And that's the nature of it. Walking the spiritual path is simple, not easy. I think the most important part of it is the realization that whatever we have is in some way a reflection of what we actually want and how we are —that we are ultimately and completely responsible for our circumstances and our experience of them.

When how we feel and function changes to attract more of what we claim we want, we will have it. We will know when we have made the shifts necessary to attract a different and better external world when we have one. No sooner and by no other means.

Since we can only attract what we want by becoming it, not by working the externals to produce it, there are some practices that can help us to shift in a way that will attract what we consciously want. I find the practices that slow and calm my thoughts provide the greatest relief and benefit. This is because my discomforts all begin with my thinking, which, when indulged in, produces feelings, often not good ones depending on my habits of thought, which then produce actions, which produce effects in the world, all of which serve as a natural and inexorable feedback loop to reveal and bring my attention to the nature and quality of my thoughts. Then, with awareness of how only I cause my own discomfort, I have the possibility of choice. Again, simple but not easy.

In each moment I choose and create my reality with my habits of thought. Only vigilant attention to them and the deliberate choice to refrain from negative ones and choose positive ones, again and again, can ultimately produce the peace and happiness I seek. That's my practice ... when I remember. Blessings and relief to you.

Phil

From: Maraya
To: Phil
Subject: Re: Post holiday blues

Thank you for your kind words of wisdom, Phil. Enjoy the rest of your spiritual vacation. *Muchas gracias amigo!*

Maraya

CHAPTER 38

Journey to the End of the Earth

*"If I ever go looking for my heart's desire again,
I won't look any further than my own back yard.
Because if it isn't there, I never really lost it to begin with."*

Noel Langley, *The Wizard of Oz*

Time was running out and I had to make good on my promise to myself. I booked a 14-day Gap Adventures' End of the Earth tour. I timed it just right. I had to leave my apartment in Recoleta for several weeks because the owner was coming home for the holidays. I dropped my extra bags at a friend-of-a-friend's tiny converted office apartment on the thirteenth floor of a building on Calle Maipu, kiddy-corner from Galerías Pacifico. It was stifling, not any kind of a place I wanted to spend too much time in.

Other than the septuagenarian couple that took the End of the Earth tour as a consolation for their cancelled Antarctica tour, I was the oldest passenger. My roommate was in her thirties—but she danced tango—so we had that in common.

We spent the first day in transit—flew to Calafate and bussed to windy El Chalten on the border between Argentina and Chile. El Chalten is the bouncing off place for those who hike or climb Cerro Chalten, which is considered one of the most technically challenging mountains in the area for mountaineers.

The next day, we hiked a dozen kilometres to Laguna de los Tres to see the three jagged granite spires: Monte Fitz Roy, Aguja Poincenot and Cerro Torre. Then we viewed the northern tip of Hielo Sur—the largest icecap not in a polar region—in Parque Nacional Los Glaciers.

The region is known for its notoriously bad weather. But, it was an unusual day for the time of year: sunny with only a moderate wind; it was a perfect day for hiking to Fitz Roy, whose peak is usually obscured by clouds. Still, it was bitterly cold and windy on the mountaintop.

Alpine flowers along the way were not unlike those in the Rockies. Yellow-flowered Calafate bushes would ripen with berries similar to Saskatoon berries found in Canada. Although one of the "elders," I lagged behind only because I wanted to stop and photograph everything. Susanne, my roommate, felt the same way. Everyone had to wait for us to catch up, but we'd have beautiful memories captured in photos long after the wrath of our fellow travellers had faded.

Back in Calafate, the temperature dropped and the sky filled with stars and a full moon. I indulged myself with a dinner of Patagonian lamb with Calafate sauce and roasted vegetables. It had been a full day. Some of my muscles complained about being woken up after many months of relative inactivity on the flat sidewalks of Buenos Aires. I was sunburned and coughing more because of the cold air exertion but it felt so good to be out in nature; I felt close to home.

Perito Moreno Glacier is one of the few glaciers in the world that is not receding. It's actually growing. It's 250 square kilometres and an average of 240 feet above the surface of Lago Argentino.

223

During our boat tour, we heard cracks but didn't see any calving —big chunks of ice breaking off. It was magnificent.

In Puerto Natales, Chile, we were warned that we couldn't take fruit or vegetables across the border. Someone did anyway, and he lied about it. He got caught and had to pay a hefty fine. I wondered, if he had told the truth, would they have just taken it away from him and not fined him? *Do you get fined for having fruit or fined for lying about it?*

Rather than the popular, five-day "W" hike, we did the "Smart W." We split the full trek into three separate day hikes to the most interesting places with meals and rest in between. Doable for all of us. I'd never done a 3-day backpacking trip and would not have signed up for one. I was thrilled with the way the tour was organized.

Our first day in Torres del Paine National Park took us to the base of the towers and campground—about seven hours. We took a catamaran and had lunch at Grey Glacier lookout point. It was a blustery day. Then, we headed back to Puerto Natales.

The next day was the longest trek of the trip to the French Valley. With two full days of hiking, and a half day on the third, the pain in my hip had miraculously worked itself out. All that fresh mountain air, activity, and being surrounded by the gorgeous natural environment felt invigorating.

Later, in the pub, I was inspired by the music; I wanted to dance. But everyone else had crashed—and were lolling around on the sofas, exhausted. There was no conversation. I felt better than I had in a long time.

I was still on supplements but I'd chosen to cheat and drink a little wine and sample spicy Mariscos Masala at a fabulous little cafe, El Living, in Puerto Natales, run by an Englishwoman. The Afrigonia dish was a fusion of African and Patagonian food, curried shrimp and scallops on saffron rice. It was well worth the cheat.

It was a long journey to Ushuaia, the southernmost city in the world. The grassy slopes were dotted with guanacas, a llama-like creature. The colony of Magellanic penguins was enchanting. We saw breaching whales while on the ferry but it happened so fast I couldn't get a photo. We drifted through the Beagle Channel and sighted the sea lions and cormorants, with the most southern lighthouse in the world in the background. I found out Highland geese mate for life. If she dies, he's so upset he doesn't eat and eventually dies. If he dies first, she finds another mate. *I love it!*

I'd done it. I'd kicked that dusty dream off my bucket list. I'd journeyed to the end of the Earth and experienced the frigid temperatures of the Land of Fire. More than any other experience during my sabbatical, exerting myself physically in the stunning natural environment made me feel most alive and energized. I realized, as much as I loved the opportunities and frenzy of Buenos Aires, I felt most at peace in the mountains. Being in Patagonia was the closest thing to being home and I felt truly blessed to live so close to the Canadian Rockies.

CHAPTER 39
A Blue Christmas

There's no place like home.

Noel Langley, *The Wizard of Oz*

Thunder rumbled through the downtown core, shaking the structures. I liked the sound of rain on the awning over the balcony. I welcomed the grey wet cool days in B.A. They suited my mood. I didn't have to feel guilty that I wasn't up and out enjoying the sunshine—because there wasn't any. The city had lost its lustre.

After feeling free in the mountains and fresh air, the apartment I was stuck in over the Christmas holidays felt downright oppressive. Mornings were the worst because I had nothing of consequence to do, except Writers' Group on Wednesdays. As much as I hated my self-imposed prison, I was reluctant to leave it. I knew I'd feel better if I got out and walked the streets, went to classes—there was really no excuse since Escuela Argentino deTango was only a block away now—but it felt like a monumental effort. So, I rolled over. *Christmas…ugh….*

I was invited to have Christmas dinner with an American family I'd met through the Newcomers' Group. Being with them helped assuage my loneliness. At least I was with a family, even if it wasn't my own. The week blurred by as I attempted to maintain some kind of regular schedule even though Estudio DNI had shut down for the holidays. Jesse and I had been awkwardly trying to re-establish some kind of friendship, and he invited me to a New Year's party at his place but I didn't want to go. I didn't want to watch him drink, do drugs, and flirt with other women. I stayed in and watched an old Rock and Roll music special on TV. So many songs reminded me of my teens—and Gerry and Nicki. I sobbed through it, releasing the overdose of nostalgia. Then I called my daughters to wish them a Happy New Year.

I woke up from a nap with a Bee Gees' song in my head: "Something's telling me I must go home." *Yes. It feels like it's time to go home.*

I thought I would be able to stay away until May but I just couldn't manage it. I was homesick. At least this year I'd forced myself to experience Christmas away. It was a stupid idea. Christmas should be spent with family. I compromised by cutting the remaining time in half. I clicked to confirm my flight home in March, and cried. Even though I had accomplished a lot, I still felt like something was missing. Whatever that "something" was that I had been blindly looking for, still eluded me. Committing to ending my adventure was somehow like admitting defeat.

From: Maraya
To: Jesse
Subject: Emails

Hey,

I shouldn't have come over, but I needed to get the last of my stuff. Thanks for storing it. It felt like right timing, but maybe I wasn't ready to see you.

So, I was about to leave and you got us into this long conversation— mostly one way—which is fine—about what you like to talk about. I

227

see that you miss having someone to talk to about that stuff. I'm trying to shut you out but I miss having someone to talk to too. I don't seem to be able to maintain relationships with any quality people (or even find many) in this town (or anywhere)—just your basic get-together-for-coffee once in a while with friends, some dancing, and an occasional session with my therapist.

One thing I always admired about you was that you were always focused and diligent about work. I'm even more lost than ever as going home time nears and I don't feel like writing at all. What the hell am I supposed to do? Phil says there is an adjustment period after going to the Casa and nothing to do but just wait...yeah, well, things feel worse than they were before I went there—and I guess I just expected too much—like a last-resort miracle of sorts. Now, no, I'm not waiting for some cataclysmic external event cuz I don't think that's the answer. I'm just depressed. You think drug dealing, I think suicide (only thinking). Anyway, not much else to do but tango I guess.

Thanks for listening.

Maraya

From: Jesse
To: Maraya
Subject: Re: Emails

Well, I was glad you did come over. I could see you were uncomfortable, which is why I did more of the talking. But, I say now what I have said before—things are what they are, and if that means you or I feel crappy and you end up in my lap because of that, then that is what there is.

I make no excuses for being selfish, fickle, undependable and, at times, inconsiderate—no excuses for my actions. And, I will always strive to be 100% honest (which doesn't mean I will volunteer any and all information), because the only reason I would lie would be to either protect someone else (which is not my job) or to preserve

228

a false image of myself, neither of which I want to do. Oddly, just about all women do not believe I can be 100% honest. Jajaja! And, just about all men think I am an idiot for trying. Oh well ... good thing I don't give a rat's ass about that.

Until next time

/j

The end of the year done and gone. I returned to my luminous apartment in Recoleta and instantly felt better. With renewed energy, I made a plan for my remaining two months. I had one more major thing to accomplish: I would master the lead. I would buckle down and take private lessons and go to Tango Queer and Practica Maria where I could practice leading. I would need that if I were to teach tango when I got home.

CHAPTER 40

Closer to Fine

There's more than one answer to these questions
Pointing me in a crooked line
And the less I seek my source for some definitive
The closer I am to fine.

Indigo Girls

I didn't want to wake up in the future and go about my life as if I'd never left. I wanted to have gone away for two years and come back to my life changed. Maybe things inside me had shifted but hadn't yet manifest in any obvious or tangible way. I had become somewhat more disillusioned, accrued more debt, and had no job. I guess that's change…not exactly what I'd hoped for. I wanted to start the new year with hope.

Instead of bleeding less, I was bleeding more. Menopause hadn't yet run its course. *Damn.* I had pages of scribbles, blathering thoughts, a blog that I felt obligated to keep up with but didn't really want to, and nothing that yet resembled a book. Just a mess of words—black on white. Paper shit.

People take vacations from their life. Sometimes it's a night of drinking and drugs—momentary oblivion; sometimes it's a holiday on a beach; sometimes it's a retreat—hoping to learn something useful, to become enlightened, to achieve joy;

sometimes it's a *milonga*. For all the effort, you just end up returning to the same place (and "know it for the first time"—or whatever that saying is) and, if you don't like it there, you leave again.

But, I could dance—damn well—now. Not only could I follow, I could lead. Sometimes I would wake up in the middle of the night rehearsing a sequence in my head. That was the nice thing about the lead—being able to "practice" it alone anywhere. It was something to focus my mind on. Learning sequences is good for the brain, and it's good for learning how elements of the dance go together; however, tango is supposed to be an improvisational dance, so those elements should be practiced to the extent that they become muscle memory. At some point, they'll just emerge naturally during the dance in response to the music. *One can hope.*

The sweet yeasty scent of freshly baked *medialunas* wafted all the way up to my top-floor apartment from the street-level *confitería* each morning, nudging me out of bed. Outside my door, I could catch a bus directly to Estudio DNI and be there in about five minutes. I was no longer taking yoga, but I was taking private tango lessons, occasionally assisting with the beginner class, and attending the *nuevo* class and *practica* on Saturday nights. I loved the contemporary music and the energy—fresh, young, open-minded; DNI attracted interesting dancers of all ages from all over the world. I would walk home afterward through dark, and often rain-drenched, streets. I was so happy to have found my "tango home" with this vibrant community. *This* is the tango, and the people, I would miss.

I continued to take classes at Escuela Argentino de Tango and was privileged to be accepted into the Masters para Maestros de Tango teacher training. Even though it was completely in Spanish, I understood most of it. That certificate signified a huge accomplishment, not just a week's worth of teacher training, but the culmination of several months of tango training.

Most residents of Buenos Aires don't dance tango. Most visitors to Buenos Aires don't dance tango. I know, hard to believe, but true. There was a time before tango that I loved other kinds of music. I still do. In B.A., I attended a Blues festival in the park and enjoyed Jazz at the Thelonious Club. I even went to a Rock concert by a Pink Floyd cover band. I was moved to tears when the lead singer began with "So,..." and the audience, in perfect English, sang along to *Wish You Were Here*. I cried again when Durga McBroom, who sang the original vocals for *Great Gig in the Sky*, came onto the stage and let loose her powerful voice. That's one concert I will never forget.

The Government of Buenos Aires is very supportive of the Arts and makes sure there are plenty of events affordable for everyone. Some of them were free. I was able to enjoy several ballets and concerts. I watched the Civic Tango Orchestra perform several times with Nestor Marconi on *bandoneon*. I had the pleasure of dancing to some of my favourite Tango Nuevo bands live at Harrods during the 2009 Tango Festival.

Even though I had not done *everything* possible in this cornucopia of a city, I had done a lot; I was full.

Now, I needed a new dance partner for the next phase of my life.

From: tangueraontour
To: pers-gx4zs-1600700414@craigslist.org
Subject: Renewed to Calgary

Hi,

I saw your ad—you're new to Calgary and looking for a dance partner? I'm in Buenos Aires but I'll be returning home to Calgary soon and I'll need a dance partner too. Where are you from?

Tanguera

From: Captain Bligh
To: tangueraontour
Subject: Re: Renewed to Calgary

Hi,

I'm from B.C., living in Calgary now. Do you Tango? I am taking lessons and want to get better. There is a good tango club here.

Captain Bligh

From: tangueraontour
To: Captain Bligh
Subject: Re: Renewed to Calgary

How cool that you tango! Of course I do—that's why I'm here in Buenos Aires. There's a good tango community in Calgary. I've been part of it for a long time. I'll look forward to talking to you more when I get home and hopefully we can dance together.

Tanguera

From: Captain Bligh
To: tangueraontour
Subject: Re: Renewed to Calgary

Sounds good. Get in touch with me when you get back to Calgary.

Captain Bligh

Ж

Linda and I walked down the promenade toward the Reserva for the last time. I enjoyed the promenade at this end of the Reserva —far from the trappings of the entrance—less populated. Locals parked their lawn chairs and picnicked at the side of the tree-lined road. We encountered a pack of dogs running around the street —mom and young ones. One pup had been struck by a vehicle and lay dead in the middle of the road, blood pooling around its head—while the others sniffed around and chased a cyclist. By now, I was used to the carnage juxtaposed with the beauty of this city.

The weather report indicated thirty-one degrees and sunny but the sky did not agree. I hadn't wanted to carry anything—like an umbrella. The trees weren't much help once the sky began to spit. There were no public buildings, no taxis, no shelter once the sky gave way full force. We still had several blocks to walk before we could find shelter in Puerto Madero. By the time we'd reached another block, it was pouring hard and we looked like a couple of wet chickens. This would have embarrassed me if it hadn't actually felt like such a relief from the heat. My summer dress clung to the front of my body, my hair was plastered to my head, and water dripped off my lashes and streamed down my face. The cork soles of my Birkenstocks were of little help in keeping me afloat. I surrendered to the freshness cleansing a layer of salt from my skin and the thin film of exhaust fumes mixed with my sweat.

It was no longer warm out. People huddled under first-floor overhangs. Jumping over puddles became pointless. We wondered if we'd even be welcome in a restaurant, but we ventured into the first one we approached. The air conditioning was on, of course it was. We ordered hot tea and shivered until we dried.

"I've decided to take a teaching job in Turkey," Linda said.

"That sounds interesting. Do you know anyone there, speak any Turkish?"

"No. I just think it would be fun to do something completely different for a couple years. Like you did."

"Well,...you never know what you're going to get. It certainly hasn't been all fun."

"Pretty much like life anywhere."

"Yeah. I guess you won't be able to take over the Writers' Group for me then. We'll have to find someone else. I really appreciate you helping me to keep it together all these months. I think it's been good for a lot of writers. We even got some published authors out of it already, that's amazing."

"It was a good idea you had."

"It was especially good for me. Gave me a weekly anchor and a support network."

"You can start another one when you get home. Do you feel ready to leave?"

"I don't feel done yet but, yes, I feel ready to leave."

"How has it ended up with you and Jesse?"

"Honestly, I don't know. We were over ages ago, yet we seem to keep clinging to each other."

"You started out as friends, maybe you'll continue to be friends."

"I guess that would be okay. Not sure what the point is in maintaining a 'friendship' with someone you're never going to see again."

"Don't say that. You don't know. Maybe he'll get his situation resolved and move back to the States, maybe you'll be back here."

"*Que será, será.*"

Soon the rain passed, the sun reappeared, and we were on our way: Linda to Turkey and me to Canada.

Ж

From: Amy
To: Maraya
Subject: Coming home!

Hi Mommy!

I'm so glad you're moving back home. I've missed you! I'm excited to hang out with you.

I feel like the pieces of my life are maybe sort of coming back together. And you coming home is the frosted pink icing on the cake. Even if it's just for now, I don't expect you to settle down forever. That's not a bad thing, it's a good thing. I admire you for doing what you want.

Sooo ... I wanted to tell you about this dream I had the other night. I thought it was really weird when I woke up, and ever since then I've been thinking about it more and more, and I think it means something but I'm not sure what.

It was you, me, Amanda, and Dad. You and Dad weren't together, but somehow the four of us were still a family. We moved into this super huge old house with three levels and tons of rooms. It was the first night we moved in and the first thing I thought was weird was that someone else's food was in the cupboards and fridge. We all found our rooms and started settling down for the night. I went to my room—which was huge! I had the eeriest feeling like it was someone else's old room but they just weren't there anymore. None of the furniture was mine and someone else's clothes were in the closet. What do you think?

Love Amy

From: Maraya
To: Amy
Subject: Re: Coming home!

Hi Honey,

236

I'm glad that you're glad that I'm coming home and that you feel better about things maybe coming together for you otherwise. Thank you for your long email. You seem more willing to talk to me. I don't feel like we've been very close but I remember when my dad died, I totally shut down. It was so hard. You're doing great. I'm looking forward to spending time with you and sharing more dreams.

I don't know what the dream means. I have a lot of dreams like that —with houses and with the family. It feels like maybe your dad and I got some healing on our relationship through dreams after he died, if that makes any sense. I think, most important, are the feelings you have during the dream (e.g., were you feeling afraid, or content, or that "weird vibe"?). Even if you don't journal much, write down the dreams you think are significant.

I'll be home at 8 p.m. on March 8th—International Women's Day.

Love you!

Mom

Ж

There was only one person I wanted to spend my last day in Buenos Aires with. Jesse and I strolled around the Japanese Gardens, a peaceful oasis in the center of the wild city I had grown to love. This was one of the many city attractions I had not yet seen. There were so many things I hadn't done. I needed something to look forward to upon my return.

"And when do you think that'll be?" Jesse asked.

"I have no idea. I think I better just stay home for a while and sort myself out. I'll have to get some work to pay for all this fooling around I've been doing for the past couple years. I'll start teaching tango and run a *practica*. Maybe I can teach or tutor English. What's next for you?"

"Well, good news,...my lawyer finally did his job. My divorce is final."

"Excellent. Congratulations!"

"Sure. But, not so great is that I still officially owe her a pile of money and she's not going to forgive it. So I still can't go back to New York, even if I had a passport. I'd get arrested.

"That sucks. Anything you can do about it?"

"Nothing right now except keep trying to get work until she chills out and gets over herself. There aren't any projects coming in here, Kaveh doesn't pay me worth shit."

"Not good, especially with the prices here—they just keep going up and up. How's the *milonga* doing?"

"Not well enough to pay the rent. Lucia's going to partner up with me and run a traditional *milonga* on Tuesdays. Her expertise should help."

"How've you been feeling?"

"Same. Still pain and I'm always tired."

"Well, you're so friggin' determined, that you're no doubt going to be fine." I'm not sure I believed myself but I wanted him to know I had confidence in him.

"Thanks. I'll miss hanging out with you. Let's make sure to keep in touch with Skype."

"Yeah, sure. That'd be good." Again, I wasn't sure I believed myself.

He took my hand and we stood on the bridge, silently enjoying the view and each other's company. There didn't seem to be much more to say.

"Well," he started, "was it worth it?"

"What? You mean coming here?"

"Yeah. Was it worth upsetting your life to come here just to upset it all over again?"

"I'm not sure. Time will tell. I'm glad I took a risk and did something crazy and survived and had some amazing experiences

238

and got some great photographs and a story to tell. I'm glad I met you."

He smiled and squeezed my hand.

We returned to his apartment to pick up my bags, then he walked me to the corner and hailed a cab. We embraced for the last time and he said, "I love you."

"I know. Goodbye, Jesse."

The taxi headed west toward the airport and I didn't look out the back window at Jesse standing alone on the curb; but, instead, toward the sky pinking up ahead. As I began my journey home and into spring, autumn was approaching the southern hemisphere. And the sun set too soon over Buenos Aires.

Is that all there is, is that all there is?
If that's all there is my friend, then let's keep dancing.

Peggy Lee

AFTERWORD

It doesn't always take ten years to complete a memoir. Mine did. Travelling and living elsewhere is a good distraction from the everyday. When you come home and back to work after a two-week holiday, you have to catch up on everything. Magnify that by 100 or so and that's what it's like to repatriate. No job, no clients. Starting over again can take years. It has.

After returning to Calgary, I taught tango lessons and hosted a practica. I had the support of my partner—the man I had connected with through Craigslist at the end of my stay in Buenos Aires. That life lasted only a few years.

Ten years after I ended my sabbatical, I visited Jesse in New York City. Yes, he's alive and has straightened out his legal situation, and most of his health issues. We've remained good friends across time and distance.

Almost ten years later, John of God was charged with over 600 counts of sexual assault and other heinous crimes. *Heavy sigh* ...

Ten years later, the Buenos Aires English Writers' Group still exists and has far surpassed the life of the writers' group I started when I returned to Calgary.

My daughters are well-adjusted, well-travelled, beautiful women inside and out. I am truly blessed.

I continue to have a love/hate relationship with tango and I miss Buenos Aires every day.

ACKNOWLEDGEMENTS

I am the combined effort of everyone I've ever known.

Chuck Palanhiuk

This book was a co-creation. It is not possible to write a memoir without first having experiences that include other people. I deeply appreciate those who found their way into this book by having made an impact upon my life during this time. I especially want to thank Jeff Milton, Nicola Elliott Lapierre, Phil Story, Bill Atkey, Kevin Carrel Footer, Bob Kochan and my daughters, Amanda and Amy, for allowing me include their words.

Thank you to the Writers Guild of Alberta for accepting me into their mentorship program, and to my mentor, Glenn Dixon for helping me complete my first draft.

Thank you to the many readers who gave me feedback on bits and pieces throughout the years through the Writer In Residence programs at the University of Calgary, the Canadian Authors Association, the Alexandra Writers' Centre Society and the City of Calgary Public Library. Thank you to the members of the Buenos Aires English Writers' Group and the NW Calgary Writers' Group. Special thanks to those beta readers who provided comments on my manuscript and the impetus to keep moving forward: Cherie Magnus, Margaret Graw, Jacquie Clarke,

Maureen McGee, Cindy Morris, Craig Copland, and Rose-Marie Jaeger. Thank you to fellow traveller and writer, Darren Flach, for kicking my ass when I was about to give up and throw it all away.

Thank you to Deborah Knott for copyediting.

Thank you to John Heerema for assisting me with my cover photo and design and for continuing to dance with me after all these years.

Thank you to my parents, Olly and Henry Chorney, for their unconditional and unending love. Without them, and my daughters, I would never have had the courage and support I needed for extended travel and the even more extended period it took to get this book out into the world. I love you.

Thank you, dear reader, for travelling this far with me in the journey. Keep dancing.

Red Arrow
67 x 76.
#8 (152.) 3½
Holiday Inn
10014 - 10161
St.
l. lees
46
705 - 9th
ave SE.

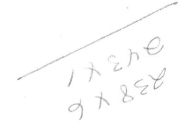

Made in the USA
Lexington, KY
16 August 2019